Praise for PLAYING WITH TRAINS

"With the empathy and insight that could come only from a true hobbyist, *Playing with Trains* takes the reader through the model railroading world and introduces us to some of the hobby's most interesting personalities. . . . I found it immensely enjoyable."
—TERRY D. THOMPSON, editor, *Model Railroader*

"This is a book that anyone can enjoy, whether passionate about model railroading or not, because it is fundamentally a human story about finding a passion, learning how to be good at it, and thrilling to the joy of sharing it with loved ones and friends."
—*Road & Track*

"[Posey] is not only a fine 'explainer' but also a first-rate stylist capable of the imaginative metaphor. And he deeply understands the minds of men our age. . . . Model railroaders will take this book to heart, but the non-modeler will also find *Playing with Trains* engaging, affectionate and eye-opening."
—*Chicago Sun-Times*

"Posey's book is the latest example of a growing number of books that could be cataloged as extreme writing, the literary answer to extreme sports."
—*USA Today*

"Posey's touching tribute to his hobby is both a sociological study and a personal journey. Anyone who has ever owned a train set or had a love affair with trains will relate."
—*Library Journal*

PLAYING WITH TRAINS

P L A Y I N G

RANDOM HOUSE TRADE PAPERBACKS / NEW YORK

WITH TRAINS

A PASSION BEYOND SCALE

Sam Posey

2005 Random House Trade Paperback Edition

Published in the United States by Random House Trade
Paperbacks, an imprint of The Random House Publishing
Group, a division of Random House, Inc., New York.

RANDOM HOUSE TRADE PAPERBACKS and colophon are
trademarks of Random House, Inc.

Originally published in hardcover in the United States
by Random House, an imprint of The Random House
Publishing Group, a division of Random House, Inc., in 2004.

LIBRARY OF CONGRESS CATALOGING-IN-PUBLICATION DATA

Posey, Sam.
    Playing with trains: a passion beyond scale / Sam Posey.
        p. cm.
    ISBN 0-8129-7126-4
    1. Railroads—Models.   I. Title.
TF197.P64 2004   625.1'9—dc22   2003070200

Printed in the United States of America

www.atrandom.com

9 8 7 6 5 4 3 2

Book design by Dana Leigh Blanchette

TO ROLF AND JOHN

TRAIN WHISEL SIGNALS

_: LongToot
.: Short Toot

.	Apply Brakes, STOP!
_ _	Relaase Brakes, PROCEED!
_ ...	Flagman go back and protect rear of train.
_ _ _ _	Flagman return from west or south.
_ _ _ _ _	Flagman return from east or north.
... _	Protect front of train.
..	Answer to any signal not otherwise provided for.
...	When standing,back up.When running,
....	Call for signals. ///// stop at next station.
_ _ ._	Approching highway or grade crossing.
_ _	Approching station,juncion,orrailroad crossing.
_ _ .	Approching a meeting or waiting point for trains.
**********	A number of short toots is a signal
	for persons or livestock on the track.

Fierce-throated beauty!
Roll through my chant with all thy lawless music,
   thy swinging lamps at night,
Thy madly-whistled laughter, echoing, rumbling
   like an earthquake, rousing all.

—WALT WHITMAN,
"TO A LOCOMOTIVE IN WINTER"

Like so many men of my generation (I was born during World War II), I fell under the spell of trains as a little boy. My father was killed in the war, and when I was six, my mother built me a layout—Lionel—that gave me a miniature universe that I could operate on my own. Speed and control: I was fascinated by both, as well as by the way they were inextricably bound together.

A generation later, when my son, John, was small, I wanted to share my passion for trains with him, which to me meant having us build a layout together. As time went by, the thing kept getting *bigger,* and it took sixteen years to finish. Along the way, I became so interested in model railroading that I went in search of the country's finest modelers to see what made them tick. I encountered a world of extremes. Extreme commitment. Extreme differences in approach to the hobby—

irreconcilable differences, in fact. These men were as tightly wound as any of the electric motors in their locomotives, and they were fiercely proud of their creations and ready to defend their turf. (As a former racing driver, I know a competitor when I see one.)

Except for describing my early enchantment with Lionel, I have kept the focus on a single scale: HO, the choice of most top modelers. I have omitted club layouts, many of which are superb, as well as large, professionally built layouts, in order to stick with the ambitions of the individual modeler.

Trains are a part of our national heritage—and modeling them is, too. It's a hobby with proven staying power because so much is involved: Imagination. Building. Tinkering. Inventing. Self-expression. It takes work to get good results, but in the end you will have mastery and control of a world of your own making.

And you get to play with trains.

Sam Posey
Sharon, Connecticut

C O N T E N T S

PART ONE

THE MIGHTY ZW

I'm pregnant," my wife, Ellen, said, and right then I knew I would be building a train layout. I saw a layout as a birthright, since playing with trains had been such a big part of my life as a kid.

When our son, John, was born in June 1982, I remember gazing at his little fingers and thinking that they were scaled down from an adult's in the same way model trains are scaled-down versions of the real thing.

My memories of trains went back to a wooden locomotive that I pushed along tracks spread out across my bedroom floor. At first, I was told to put the tracks away each night, but as I began to make the configurations more complex, I was allowed to leave everything in place, sometimes for weeks at a time. I built stations with my blocks, stuffed books under the rug to make hills, and designed loops that tunneled under my bed.

When I was four I ran into the living room Christmas morning to discover a locomotive that was made of metal and painted dark blue. A large key lay next to it. My mother showed me how a lever on top of the cab kept the spring mechanism from unwinding until I had the engine positioned on the tracks and its three passenger cars hooked up. Once released, the train accelerated down the straight, then flipped over at the first curve, leaving the wheels spinning in the air until the spring unwound. If I didn't wind it quite so much, the engine stayed on the tracks but expired after a lap, leaving me wishing I had wound it *just a little tighter.* This was an improvement over my wooden trains, which I had to push, but like most boys my age, I already longed for the next step: electric trains.

Lionel trains.

The word *Lionel* was magic. My Lionel train layout in our house in New York gave me the first inklings of an identity I could call my own. For first grade, I was enrolled at Buckley, a school for boys, where you were either a train guy or a fort guy— no one had both trains *and* a fort. The forts were based on medieval castles. The most elaborate had drawbridges, portcullises, battlements, operating catapults, and moats that held real water. Lead soldiers could be arranged as attackers and defenders. But the only way to play with a fort was to move things around by hand, which recalled the effort that had gone into operating my wooden trains. The moment you sat back to watch, the action stopped. Trains were different.

Once it was established that you were a train guy and not a fort guy, the next choice was between the two major manufacturers of toy trains, Lionel and its archrival, American Flyer. The differences were few but important. American Flyer's engines and cars had a cheap, plastic feel, and their couplers were ungainly hooks that did not even attempt to look like the real thing. Lionel, by contrast, had authentic couplers, and big, solid locomotives and cars. It was their track that was flawed: instead of a realistic two-rail system, Lionel had three rails. The third rail provided the current from the transformer and simplified the wiring of a complex layout, but it looked awful.

None of us kids had made the choice between Lionel and American Flyer ourselves. That was left to our parents. When we argued over our trains, we were doing more than defending their particular features, we were upholding the judgment of people we loved and believed in. My mother had chosen Lionel, and any criticism of Lionel was, to me, a criticism of her.

The name *Lionel* came from Joshua Lionel Cowen, who had been building toy trains since 1900. Cowen was an inventor who knew his way around electrical devices and manufacturing techniques. He was also an aggressive businessman. He battled his first big competitor, the Ives Corporation, by depicting their trains as weak and flimsy, comparing their least expensive models with his top-of-the-line stuff—without mentioning the price difference. He took out ads showing Lionel track supporting more than one hundred pounds while another brand's broke apart under just twenty.

Cowen combined showmanship with a knack for attracting celebrities. He arranged for Jackie Gleason to do a TV skit in which a Lionel engine towed a flatcar—which carried a drink— out to Gleason on the set. Pope Pius XII, in full ecclesiastical garb, posed with Lionel equipment in the Vatican. Roy Rogers, Tommy Dorsey, and Johnny Weissmuller all appeared with the trains in publicity shots. One of Cowen's few frustrations came from trying to establish a connection between trains and baseball. In 1950 he managed to hire Joe DiMaggio to host a TV series, *The Lionel Clubhouse,* which aired briefly on NBC but didn't last.

Cowen lived into his eighties, and his long career spanned both world wars and the Great Depression. Throughout these decades of uncertainty, he offered stability: a world to escape into in which everything was always under control. The trains, and all the Lionel accessories, did what they were told. Semaphores saluted as engines passed, plastic cows shuffled aboard cattle cars, coal rattled down chutes. Industries thrived—including Cowen's own, which grossed a whopping $33 million in 1953, Lionel's best year.

Cowen's greatest strength was that he understood the mythology of the American family. He used his catalogs to create a world in which Father knew best. Father's role was to watch indulgently as Son operated the trains. Son was destined to assume the traditions of hard work and fair play that had been passed down from generation to generation. Mother and Little Sister (she was always younger), if they appeared in a picture at all, were in the background as an adoring audience, along with the family's dog, which was typically a Scottie or small collie. Everyone was always smiling, and enough love was beaming around to power the trains.

Cowen's catalogs shamelessly exploited parental emotions. Fathers, wearing tweed jackets and smoking pipes, were shown with their arms around their boys, as both father and son gazed fondly at the trains. Another of Cowen's favorite concepts— illustrated by a picture of a boy sleeping with a Lionel locomotive on his pillow—was to suggest to parents that their boy fell to sleep dreaming of trains. In the years after World War II, Cowen turned Christmas into a marketing event for his products. He made Christmas and Lionel so inseparable you couldn't be sure which came first, the trains or the tree.

Cowen's propaganda meant little to me because, as a kid, I never saw the Lionel catalogs. My mother bought my trains at FAO Schwarz, a large New York toy store, and put them under our Christmas tree, unwrapped. She never pretended the trains came from Santa. Cowen's glorification of the father and son relationship, even had I known about it, would have had little meaning for me, because my father had been killed when I was only eleven months old. He had seen me just once, on a brief leave after D-day, before he was transferred to the Pacific, where a kamikaze struck his ship; his body was never found. As for brothers and sisters with whom to share Cowen's idea of the wholesome fun of trains, I had none until my mother remarried years later.

But the biggest deviation from the perfect Lionel family was that a woman, my mother, wired the layout. She may have been trying to make up for some of what I missed by not having a father, but she genuinely liked trains—and other things that were unusual for a woman at that time. She studied with a professional cabinetmaker and had a shop of her own where she built miniature furniture and refinished antiques. During the war, she drove a truck (stick shift!) up and down the hills of San Francisco. She loved cars and considered herself duty-bound to take any one she owned out for at least one run at top speed.

If someone asked me if I had a train set, I would regard the questioner with scorn. A train *set* appeared at Christmas, after which it was put away. What I had, what my mother had designed and commissioned a carpenter to build, was a *layout*. It was permanent. Mine even had a room of its own, on the same floor as the living room. It was part of the action. In fact, in a house that didn't yet have a TV, my train room often *was* the action.

Stepping through the doorway, you were confronted by two tiers of tracks that stretched from one wall to the other. You either stayed by the door (the choice of most grown-ups) or ducked under the tracks, emerging in the center of the layout, next to the controls. Trains could be run on the lower level, which was wide enough for the main line, plus sidings and accessories, or the upper level, a narrow shelf with space for just one track. Ramps connected the levels. Standing inside the layout, with one train going clockwise along the lower level and another running counterclockwise on the upper, was like being at the center of a universe. At night, the lights of the trains orbited around me as if I were the nucleus of an atom.

Lionel's line of trains and accessories suffered from a split personality because they tried to look like scale models but work like toys. A passenger train appeared authentic moving along a straight—until it reached one of Lionel's turns, which were so sharp that if they had existed in real life, negotiating them would have derailed the engine and flattened the passengers against the walls of the cars. The street lamps, too, looked good until you realized that in order to accommodate actual lightbulbs, they were wildly out of scale. My station was architecturally accurate, but it was painted garishly in red and green in an obvious bid for the Christmas market.

The biggest challenge to realism had less to do with appearance than awkwardness of operation. At the gate crossing hut, the door snapped open and the guard popped out like a jack-in-the-box. Plastic cows being shunted aboard a cattle car frequently tipped over, jamming at the door. Lionel's smoke was produced by a pill dropped into the engine's smokestack, but the pills were too small, and engines raced along emitting a pale effluvium that was less convincing than my mother's Kool. The coal-dumping car would get stuck in middump, then revive, hurling coal across the layout. The log loader's conveyor belt made a grinding noise as loud as a garbage disposal.

One sound Lionel got dead right, however, was the whistle of their steam locomotives. It even trailed off hauntingly—in accordance with the Doppler effect—as the locomotive went away from you. Cowen's designers achieved the lonely, evocative sound with a fan that blew air through miniature organ pipes.

I couldn't do much about the third rail, or the hairpin turns, or the eccentric accessories, but when it came to operating the trains the degree of realism was up to me. Each spring, my family traveled by train to Florida, and those trips gave me a chance to see how things were done by real railroads. I took what I observed and applied it to my layout. I eased my engines away from the station. I kept them to sensible speeds on the straights, slowed well in advance of the curves, and coasted into the station, always coming to a smooth stop.

I also observed the correct whistle signals for each situation, guided by a typed card that was placed next to the controls. It was a railroader's Morse code: a short toot was a dot, a long one a dash. *Dot:* apply brakes and stop. *Dash, dash:* release brakes and proceed. *Dash, dash, dot, dash:* approaching highway or grade crossing. One long blast: approaching station.

Sometimes, however, all this conscientious operation and righteous whistle-blowing was just too much, and I'd crank the throttle wide open and watch a train go hurtling down a straight and, like my old windup engine, flip over at the first curve it came to. Or I would position a herd of the plastic cows on the tracks, then plow through them, meanwhile blowing the whistle like mad. I also enjoyed crashing into the back of a hapless freight that had stopped along the main line, scattering boxcars across the tracks. I knew Lionel's equipment was tough and could take quite a beating without showing a scratch, but I made sure nothing ever took the big fall from the layout to the floor.

I saw trains as serious business. On my visits to FAO

Schwarz, I studied their layout, imprinting the track plan in my mind and memorizing the placement of the accessories. I was already doing badly at school, the first intimations that my academic career (if it could be called that) was headed for trouble, and my train room had become a sanctuary, a place where I was in control, away from the bewilderment of the classroom. If I pulled the lever for a switch, a green light would blink off and a red one come on, and from across the room I would hear a buzz and know that the switch was now set for a curve instead of a straight and that a train would be turning off the main line and climbing the ramp to the upper level. I didn't have to see it, I knew it was happening.

I could couple and uncouple cars without touching them. I could load and unload logs, cattle, milk cans, and coal. I could raise or lower our bascule bridge. I could leave a train running and go down the hall to the living room to chat with my mother, and when I came back, the train would be circling the layout exactly as I had left it. Remote control; it was one of Joshua Cowen's most cherished concepts, relentlessly promoted as instilling in young boys a sense of responsibility for their actions. As Ron Hollander wrote in *All Aboard!,* his history of Lionel, "Remote control became symbolic of the button-pushing and emotional distancing that would be required of men in the real world."

Most of the switching and activating of accessories was a simple choice of on or off, but when it came to controlling the trains themselves you had forward or reverse plus the choice of how fast you wanted to go. You could make incremental adjustments in speed by moving the twin throttles of what Lionel called the transformer. On my layout the transformer was the 275-watt ZW, the biggest Lionel made.

The ZW was a black cube, rounded at the edges, with a large

L for Lionel on the top and cone-shaped protrusions extending horizontally from either side. The cones were the throttles, and sticking up out of each was a plastic lever that I could move with just the slightest pressure. The ZW had the look of something pagan, a dark eminence through which electric power flowed in mysterious ways. Even my mother had no idea what went on inside. But to me the real magic of the ZW was that something happened in there that took my idea of how fast I wanted my train to go and turned it into movement many feet away. To Joshua Cowen, this was remote control. To me, it was something more: *power without effort*—the sensation I had sought without success back in the days of my wooden trains, and something I have pursued in one form or another for most of my life.

I was nine when my mother married Dr. Samuel W. Moore, a man who had worked his way up from the red clay of rural North Carolina to a position of distinction in the medical world. After the wedding, we moved out of the house into an apartment, which didn't have room enough for the layout. The tracks were pulled up, the equipment put in boxes, the big table dismantled; the place that had made me feel that I was at the center of a universe went back to being an ordinary room.

My mother assured me that the layout would be resurrected in the new house we were about to build in Sharon, Connecticut, about one hundred miles north of New York. Two years later, the house was finished, and I began immediately to lobby for my new layout. To my surprise, my stepfather volunteered to build it. I was excited. Carpentry was a hobby of his, and while he didn't have my mother's skills, he was good at making things that were robust and built to last.

When the day came to build the layout, he was ready with an

idea for how to do it. Our new house was low and modern, with roof overhangs that extended six feet beyond the walls, and when the rafters were installed, the underside of each was sawed off to create a flat soffit. A long, skinny triangle was left as waste, and since these pieces looked as if they could be useful for something, the construction crew had stacked them in a pile, where my stepfather had spotted them.

"We'll use these as the legs," he announced, and moments later we were dragging them down the stairs to the basement, to a dark room where it had been decided my layout would go. Working hastily, Dr. Moore began nailing the triangular legs to sheets of thin plywood, spacing the legs so far apart that the plywood sagged between them. He installed the legs with the wide end at the top, which to me looked upside down. My dismay grew as the table took shape; my stepfather, however, didn't notice.

When he finished, I was left alone to stare at what he had built. My first thought was to disguise as much of it as possible with scenery. I had wanted some scenery anyway—the wood wasn't even painted, and I longed for the new layout to look more like a real place. I had hoped for mountains; now I *needed* them. As for how they would be built, my stepfather made it clear I was on my own.

In the days of the windup locomotive, a mountain about eighteen inches long had straddled the tracks. Trees and streams were painted on the outside, and the inside was gray, like a tunnel. It had been made of papier-mâché, and I thought this would be a good material to use for my mountains now. I lugged a bag of flour, stacks of newspapers, and several buckets of water down to the basement and began trying to make papier-mâché. Hours later, surrounded by damp lumps of flour and soggy newspapers, I realized I couldn't do it. Papier-mâché was out.

Then I had an inspiration: burlap! Our house was on a farm,

and seed was delivered regularly to the barn in burlap bags, which assured me a plentiful supply. Build wood supports, I thought, curved like mountains, then stretch the burlap over the supports. I wasn't old enough to be allowed to use power tools, so I began cutting the mountain outlines by hand with a coping saw. This was tedious work, and it didn't help that the blades kept breaking. I needed a new plan and soon settled for nailing leftover scraps of wood together into a wobbly arc. I made several of these arcs, fastening one end of each to the wall and the other end to the table. The next step was to stretch the burlap over the wood.

I didn't have a staple gun, so I hunted around and found some tacks. But as I hammered them into the arcs, the wood scraps broke apart. All I could do was drape the burlap from arc to arc, which gave it the look of a circus tent, not a mountain. Discouraged, I unpacked some of my old track and set up a rudimentary loop. I hooked up the ZW, which looked smaller than I remembered it. I dug out an engine and placed it on the tracks.

Speeding down the straight, it porpoised across the sagging plywood. When the locomotive entered the mountain, I could see it through the weave of the burlap, a ghost with a bright headlight.

The layout was a failure.

I was eleven when the layout failed, and the next two years saw me taking big steps toward growing up. Soon the trains seemed to belong to a childhood I was leaving behind. When I played a game with my new friend John Whitman, it was Monopoly or Ping-Pong, or one of our own invention involving model cars. And when our family took a trip, we no longer went by train—we flew.

I soon found myself with two young brothers, Nick and David. My mother decided they should have a layout, just as I had, but instead of Lionel she bought them trains built by Märklin, a German firm. Märklin's trains were smaller than those of Lionel or American Flyer, but they were higher quality. Märklin track was also more realistic. The curves were gentle, and the ties were embedded in a simulated gravel roadbed. Märklin used a third rail, but unlike Lionel's it was cleverly disguised.

My mother located the new layout upstairs, in a sunny play-room complete with a TV. From the beginning, the TV competed with the trains for my brothers' interest. Within a couple of years the Märklin equipment, neglected, joined my old Lionel stuff in storage. But I barely noticed. I had become enthralled by cars—and competition. Automobile racing became the passion of my teenage years, then my profession.

Racing was a natural extension of what had attracted me to trains. It offered the same control of a mechanical object. It allowed me to unleash power that was extravagantly greater than the effort I made to set it in motion. Crack the throttle of the ZW and the locomotive moved; depress the accelerator of a Ferrari and the car leapt forward.

I had few second thoughts about racing, despite the danger, until my wife, Ellen, became pregnant with John. By then, I was thirty-eight and had climbed as far up the racing ladder as I was going to get. All at once, I now saw risk everywhere, even though the sport had become much safer in recent years. I decided to quit. I wanted to stick around to watch John grow up.

My idea of what it would be like to be a father was hazy—except for one thing: I had a vivid image of myself as a Lionel Dad.

My mother had stored my old trains in neatly labeled cartons in the basement of her house, and at first, I looked forward to seeing them again after so long. As Christmas approached, however, I began to have misgivings. My memories of the trains were tainted by their connection to the upside-down legs and drooping burlap of my failed layout, and I began to think that what I really wanted was to start with a clean slate.

Lionel was still making trains. Or, rather, following Cowen's death in 1965, they had leased the name to General Mills, which had in turn farmed out the manufacturing to one of their subsidiaries, a company named Fundimensions. Judging from the product, Fundimensions was doing a good job, but something beyond their control had gone awry. The Lionel trains of my era had been modeled after real ones, in a time when trains, especially to kids like me, were still the most glamorous and exciting things on the planet. Fundimensions was producing those same trains, but now they looked dated. I thought John should have something different, although I didn't know what.

To me, buying trains had always meant a trip to FAO Schwarz, but now I was living a two-hour drive away. I looked for hobby shops in the Yellow Pages and found one listed in Canaan, Connecticut, which was less than thirty minutes north of Sharon. Canaan—the Promised Land! I drove up. After the glamor of FAO Schwarz, Berkshire Hills (as the hobby shop was called) looked small and run-down, an unlikely place to find trains that would measure up to the ambitions I was beginning to have for John's new layout.

I opened the door and stepped in. A bell tinkled somewhere in the back, and a shadowy form emerged and stood behind the counter. I was acutely aware of being the only customer, maybe the only one for the last several hours, or even days, and I felt the weight of intense scrutiny. A glass case filled with locomotives caught my eye. Stepping over to it, I relaxed; the close study of the locomotives was, surely, appropriate behavior and wouldn't betray my ignorance.

On the shelves were perhaps fifty steam engines and diesels. About the size of the Märklin locomotives, these were, like Märklins, more like models than toys. I looked closer. The locomotives were resting on track that had . . . just two rails!

Emboldened by my excitement, I began asking questions. I was told that this was HO (pronounced *H-oh*). HO wasn't a company, it was a *scale:* 1:87, in which an eighth of an inch equaled roughly one foot. Unlike the single-brand shopping offered by Lionel, HO equipment was manufactured by a variety of small firms. The track came from one company, the transformer from another, and so forth. The shop was crowded with supplies such as balsa wood, dowels, sandpaper, and glue, as well as kits for structures, but on that first visit I didn't grasp the significance of this, which was that people with HO layouts rarely bought their accessories—they made them.

I took home a power pack, which was what a transformer was called in the language of HO; enough curves and straights for a simple oval; and a little steam engine that, thanks to a felicitous arrangement of its boiler, headlight, and cow catcher, seemed to be smiling. The bill? Less than $50. HO was a steal.

The next day, I bought a four-by-eight-foot sheet of plywood, painted it green, and trimmed the edges with strips of pine. On Christmas Eve, I laid the track, then hooked up the power pack and tested the engine. It ran perfectly.

Most people view model train layouts from above. On Christmas morning, John crawled into the living room, so he first saw his from eye level. His gaze fixed on the locomotive and remained there as it did lap after lap. The longer he watched, the more intrigued he seemed to be. He gurgled and flapped his arms as the train approached, and followed it intently as it moved away. The locomotive didn't have a whistle, so I made some tooting noises and John laughed.

The next Christmas, John was eighteen months old, and I thought his layout should be more than a piece of green plywood. He was starting to walk and talk; he should have *scenery*. I bought some issues of a magazine called *Model Railroader* and saw that many of the HO layouts they featured depicted the American West in the era of the old mining towns, around 1890. It was almost as if HO modelers could think of nothing else.

Neither could I. All at once, I found myself daydreaming about craggy peaks, rushing streams, high wooden bridges, and a town with a dusty and rutted Main Street. I wanted saloons and maybe a jail, with a dangerous hombre or two lounging outside. Lionel had seemed dated, yet here was a world fully fifty years older that struck me as just right. Mountains, however, cropped up everywhere in my imagined scenes, and I didn't know any more about building them now than in the old burlap days.

This time, however, power tools were allowed. Adjacent to our house was a stable that we had converted into a studio and woodworking shop. Among the many tools in the shop was an electric jigsaw—exactly what I had needed to cut out the arcs for the burlap mountains.

I started by making a sketch of a mountain at either end of the layout, with a valley in between. Refining this basic idea, I downgraded one mountain into a hill and exaggerated the ruggedness of the other. The valley between them deepened into a chasm. I drew tunnel portals and settled on a track plan with two loops, one inside the other. As the drawing took shape, I felt confident. The frenzy of burlap and papier-mâché belonged to another time.

When I began to build, the jigsaw cut through piece after piece of plywood. *Zzzzzzzuuuhhhzzzz* . . . the saw felt solid and free of vibration; it chewed through the wood with power to spare. Soon the pieces were fastened to the original green board and tied to one another with spacers. I laid the track and ran a locomotive. Its disappearance into the mountain added dimensions of mystery and anticipation that were not there when you could follow the train the whole way around.

I fastened legs to the corners of the platform, which raised the layout so that John could operate the controller standing up. The shop was unheated, and on the days when it was cold enough for us to see our breath, John and I would pretend we were puffing like locomotives.

Two trains could be operated independently, one on each loop. John regarded the inner loop, with the station and the tunnels, as his. We had acquired a cheap switch engine that had an elastic band (rather than gears) driving the wheels, and he ran it lap after lap at full speed, until the band snapped.

John was four when our daughter, Judy, was born. We now had the perfect Lionel family, minus the dog, the pipe, and the Lionel trains. The next summer, I began designing our new house. I had help from my brother David, who had just become a licensed architect. As we developed the plans, David and I made sure that the basement had a place for a big layout. When we moved in I placed the four-by-eight-foot table, with its plywood Rockies, in the center of this area, and there it sat for a couple of years.

By now, John was in second grade. He saw the basement primarily as a venue for racing his tricycle. When I occasionally mentioned enlarging the layout, he cautioned me not to build anything that would obstruct the bike course. Judy, now three, also liked to ride in the basement, especially when she was able to frustrate John by blocking him when he attempted to pass her. Maybe I had been brainwashed by Joshua Cowen's attitude toward girls, but somehow I couldn't see Judy caring much about the trains. I began to understand that if we were going to have a layout, at least for now it would be because *I* wanted it.

"I've had an idea for the layout," I said at supper one evening. No one as much as looked up. When the meal was over, I went

to my drafting table in our new studio and drew a broad platform, waist high, with plywood sides extending to the floor, oc-
cupying the unused space between the path of the tricycles and
the foundation wall. Its footprint resembled a boomerang. The
next morning I called my friend Dick Coon, the contractor who
had built our house, and he sent over one of his carpenters, Bill
Berry. Bill finished the platform in a week.

Built on a framework of two-by-fours and sheathed in three-
quarter-inch plywood, it was handsome and sturdy—far better
than anything I might have hoped for when my stepfather had
built my ill-fated layout. As John and I gazed across this plywood veld, I could see that his interest in trains was being re-
vived. We began to talk excitedly about what we might build,
and everything seemed possible, including ideas that had nothing to do with the Old West.

I had read about something called the Nullarbor Straight, in
southern Australia. It was part of the New South Wales Railway's transcontinental line that ran from Sydney to Perth. Crossing the hot, barren Nullarbor Plain, the straight was three
hundred miles long, the longest straight *thing* anywhere in the
world. It was so boring for the men running the locomotives that
to keep them from falling asleep, the railroad installed a device
that the engineer had to reset every ninety seconds or an alarm
would sound and the brakes would slam on.

I described the Nullarbor Straight to John, and both of us
began fantasizing about it. We envisioned the precise geometry
of the parallel lines of steel and the way a train ran on and on
until the idea of movement lost its points of reference. At 80
mph, a train might appear to be hovering above the tracks, mo-
tionless, while the desert flew by. We wanted that for our layout,
and a quick glance across that expanse of plywood made you
think that you might actually be seeing the Nullarbor Plain.

Then I did a little math, and our dreams dissolved. Reproduced in HO scale, the Nullarbor Straight would be over three miles long. From one edge of our platform to the other was just twenty-two feet.

So we couldn't have a huge straight. The next image that came to mind was of broad, sweeping *curves,* perhaps along a river like the Hudson. On the earlier layouts, the turns had been made with manufactured sections of track that came already curved, the radius being whatever the manufacturer had decided upon. Lionel's turns had been absurdly tight, Märklin's not so bad, and HO's best of all—but still unrealistically sharp. The solution was a product, Flextrak, I had seen at the hobby store. As its name suggested, Flextrak could be bent to any radius you chose. Available in sections thirty-six inches long, it relaxed the rigidity inherent in track planning. More important, it transformed a toy into something with the potential of a scale model.

As I saw it, Flextrak meant a commitment to a degree of realism from which there could be no turning back. For hours, I fussed at my drafting table with arcs and tangents, trying to wring from them a geometry that was both elegant and original. In the end, however, I had to settle for a plan that was conceptually identical to the four-by-eight-foot layout: a pair of concentric loops connected to each other by spur tracks. But this time there was room for embellishments, and I was able to add a loop for Judy, a couple of sidings, plus two half loops that would allow trains to reverse direction. Our curves would have spiral easements, which in the world of real railroads were designed to create smooth transitions off the straights by having the turns begin gently and tighten up progressively. And they would be banked—just like the real thing.

At the same time, I started to plan the scenery. After our flirtations with long straights and sweeping curves, the Old West had reasserted itself as the motif of choice. We owned a book about Colorado by one of the masters of nineteenth-century photography, William Henry Jackson. The pictures were in black and white, which abstracted and simplified the landscape, making it seem easier to model. I studied the Western layouts featured in *Model Railroader* and compared them with Jackson's landscapes. I was impressed by the realism the modelers were able to achieve and wondered if our layout would ever look like any of theirs. After all, I had yet to complete even one mountain. But a possible solution had occurred to me: blue foam.

Blue foam is a dense Styrofoam product that was developed by Dow Chemical for use as insulation. I was familiar with it because my interest in architecture had led me to start a small company that designed and built houses in our area, and we used a lot of it. The foam was sold in rigid, extremely lightweight sheets two feet wide, two inches thick, and eight or ten feet long. Stacks of the stuff were commonplace at our construction sites.

One day I loaded up several of the blue sheets and brought them home. To my delight, a handsaw with a narrow blade ripped through the foam with the ease of a power saw cutting wood. I didn't know what the next step would be, but I sensed that using this foam, somehow, could be a way to build our mountains.

In real life, of course, the mountains are there before the railroads, and railroad surveyors plot a route through them, often enduring great hardship. But in model railroads, the track comes first, and I had noticed that in many layouts the mountains just popped up wherever space remained between the rails—hardly the majestic ranges I envisioned. I hoped to do better. I also intended to avoid steep grades.

Nineteenth-century American steam locomotives, for all

their mechanical muscularity, usually had only four driving wheels—and these were steel wheels running on steel rails, each wheel having a contact patch about the size of a dime. With ample power but so little grip, these early engines struggled to haul even light loads up any grade steeper than 3 percent, which was the limit I set for ours.

My first step was to scale up the diagram and trace it onto the plywood tabletop. Then I cut long, narrow strips of Homasote (a product made from compressed paper) and screwed them to the table. The Homasote would deaden the hollow sound the trains made as they ran across the table. Glued on top of the Homasote was cork, which I sanded to bank the turns. Then came the rails.

Scaling, cutting, gluing, sanding—it sounded as if I were following steps from Layout Building 101, which in turn suggested that I might actually know what I was doing. But I had no plan, unless wanting something badly enough was a kind of plan in itself. And I wanted the tracks to come out right. Time after time, I tore out hours of work in order to make small improvements. But I didn't mind. Not only was I finding that I enjoyed the work itself, I realized that John's impression of me—and of the way I thought things should be done—was being formed, right now, by the care and patience I was showing.

I had never had an agenda for how I should be as a dad, but here all at once was a way of communicating values. That is what Cowen's tweed jacket and pipe were all about, of course. No shortcuts for Dad. Dad did things right. Dad was patient. No swearing!

I put in many hours on the roadbed before laying even a single piece of track. Delayed gratification! It, too, was good. John, in his pajamas and bathrobe, worked with me, and I could almost feel the Message seeping through the terry cloth.

A good roadbed, I knew, was essential to the success of real railroads. I didn't mind that ours was taking far more time than I would have imagined—in fact, the work made what I was doing seem more real and authentic. But I knew that this work, and the time, would mean little even to me in the end. The finished layout would succeed only to the extent its illusions succeeded.

I first saw pictures of John Allen's layout in Monterey, California, just as I was beginning to install our new Flextrak. The photographs, mostly taken by Allen himself, illustrated a book about the layout written by an early editor of *Model Railroader,* Linn H. Westcott. Allen's layout was the size of a three-car garage, but it looked as if it existed without any borders at all. Allen had achieved a degree of realism beyond my imagining.

His mountains started right on the floor and reached to the ceiling. His valleys led deep into the mountains, blending seamlessly into a painted backdrop that extended the view to peaks that appeared twenty miles away. His 400-foot-long main line (almost 7 scale miles) traversed a torturous route, crossing 150 bridges and climbing 30 inches (260 scale feet) from the valley floor to the highest mountain pass. Trains were everywhere, as well as buildings and towns, but they were overwhelmed by the landscape.

I studied that book for hours. The closer I looked, the less real—in a literal sense—Allen's modeling looked and the more evocative—in an emotional sense—it became. Many of his photographs were of vistas that looked distinctly apocalyptic, like something Albrecht Dürer might have painted. Allen's geology was strictly freelance, and he had conjured up an unremittingly harsh world. Vegetation was sparse, and many of his trees were dead.

Consider the book's cover. It was a shot of a freight train pulling away from a station deep in a valley, a place where you knew the sun rarely shone. The locomotive's headlight was glowing faintly in the gloom. Details drew you in and made you inhabit the scene. A one-legged man hobbled along on crutches. A few shacks occupied a narrow strip of land between the tracks and a stream, which was stagnant, suggesting a tributary of the Styx. A second train, hauling logs, waited above on a track overhung by a menacing cliff.

Allen called his railroad the Gorre and Daphetid, which you were supposed to pronounce "gory and defeated." Other puns in this vein included a mountain called Cold Shoulder, a town called Squawbottom (at the base of Scalp Mountain), and the Akinbak Range. Puns weren't an affliction peculiar to John Allen; they were endemic to modelers of the 1950s, who perhaps worried that they might be regarded as taking their basement hobby too seriously. It was one thing to be a Lionel Dad, quite another to be known as a grown man who played with trains. And yet that is exactly what John Allen was.

Born in 1913, he was orphaned at six and sent to live with an aunt. A case of rheumatic fever weakened his heart and kept him out of World War II. When the war ended, Allen was living frugally off a modest inheritance in Monterey. Able to get by without a job, he decided to build a small HO layout, which he soon expanded. In 1948, he entered a contest sponsored by *Model Railroader* and won the prize for best structure. The building itself—a two-stall engine house—was unremarkable; what caught your eye was the way Allen had streaked it with chalk and paint to produce a weathered look. He even simulated pigeon droppings. The aging engine house was a departure from the crisp, clean models that were characteristic of the time, and it struck a nerve with other modelers. A weathering front swept through the hobby. As Linn Westcott wrote, "The engine house propelled John Allen into the model railroad limelight."

He began the final version of the Gorre and Daphetid in 1954, when he moved to a ranch house at 9 Cielo Vista Terrace. Unmarried and working mostly alone, he was able over the next eighteen years to concentrate on model railroading as no one had before. As the layout took shape, he documented each step in photographs. Allen had majored in art and photography at UCLA, and his brooding pictures became a kind of trademark, contributing over time to the myth of a reclusive genius.

In 1970, Andy Sperandeo (later to become editor of *Model Railroader*) was a first lieutenant in the army, serving at Fort Ord, just north of Monterey. Andy was interested in model trains and when he heard that Allen invited enthusiasts to operate the layout with him, he became a regular visitor to Cielo Vista Terrace.

"The operating sessions were on Tuesday evenings," Andy recalls. "There would be seven or eight of us, and we'd start by having coffee upstairs. Living by himself made John welcome the company, and he did most of the talking. He'd talk for forty-five minutes straight. And it wasn't all about trains, either, because he was well-read and interested in a wide range of subjects.

"When we went down to the basement, it was cool at first, but with that many people down there, things soon warmed up. He wanted you to focus on running the trains, and he insisted that you pay attention. One week, he thought there was too much talking, so the next Tuesday he hid a pocket tape recorder in the ceiling. After the session, he played it back for us to make his point. The next week, we were pretty quiet, and when the tape was played all you could hear was John cursing one of his locomotives."

Allen appeared enigmatically in some of his own photographs, a Hitchcockian presence, always looking at something he was working on, never the camera. In the pictures, we see that he wore glasses and was overweight. A heart attack in the mid-1960s left him short of breath and easily tired. As he worked on the last stretch of track to complete his masterpiece, he was aware that he might not live to see it finished. He didn't. John Allen died of a second heart attack, in January 1973, at the age of fifty-nine.

Ten days later, some friends from Allen's regular operating group gathered to run the railroad and to discuss what could be done to preserve it. An hour after they left, a fire broke out, gutting the house and destroying the layout. According to the Linn Westcott book, a private investigator identified the cause of the fire as a rarely used furnace that was located under the layout and speculated that the furnace wasn't properly vented. Not everyone was satisfied by this explanation. Some insisted that Allen had actually *planned* the fire because he didn't want the layout to survive him. Andy Sperandeo disagrees. "People have a hard time believing that it was an accident, that's all," he told me.

"I want us to build scenery like this," I said to John as we studied pictures of John Allen's layout, "something good enough to be published in a magazine."

I expected him to say he was sure we could, and I was surprised when he shook his head.

"Bet we can't do it, Dad," John said. He didn't mean, literally, to bet money, he didn't think that way, but I liked the idea.

"I'll bet," I said. "How much?"

John hesitated. His allowance was a quarter.

"A dollar?" he said.

"Deal." Trying to win a bet with my son seemed less presumptuous, somehow, than trying to get a layout published, especially one that was barely begun.

I was absorbed by thoughts for the layout, but I had little practical knowledge and ran into trouble as soon as I tried to lay the rails. Unlike the preassembled curved sections, Flextrak was custom-fitted to each turn. The rails were nickel silver, which made them difficult to cut through. I tried a hacksaw, but the blade just skidded across the surface. Then I saw an ad for something called a Xuron, an aggressive-looking pair of pliers designed specifically for this job. The Xuron just sounded tough, so I ordered one, and when it arrived its sharp jaws bit through the nickel silver with ease.

Next, I had a tough time fastening the track to the roadbed. The ties had holes predrilled in their centers, and the idea was to hammer a small headless nail—a brad—through the hole and into the sub-roadbed. I found that even a little tack hammer was too big for this delicate job, so I tried forcing the brads in with a pair of needle-nosed pliers. But often the brads just fell over between the ties. My solution was to wait for John to return from school. His small fingers were able to grip the brads, and then I was able to push them in, straight, with the pliers.

Naturally, each time we installed a new section, we felt com-

pelled to check it out with a locomotive. And just because one locomotive worked all right, it didn't guarantee that another
would, so further testing was invariably deemed necessary. Often
we ran through our whole roster before declaring ourselves satisfied.

And our roster kept expanding. Although John and I would
visit Berkshire Hills fully intending to limit ourselves to utilitar-
ian supplies such as cork or Flextrak, invariably we were drawn
to the glass case and there, each time, was a locomotive too exciting to resist. I thought that to be consistent with our Old West
theme we should buy only steam engines, but on one visit John
became enamored of a bright yellow and silver Rio Grande
diesel. A diesel? That didn't belong in my scenario. Then I remembered that Emerson had once said, "A foolish consistency is
the hobgoblin of little minds." It was enough, I decided, that the
Rio Grande was a railroad based in the West.

The new locomotive ran so well that other diesels soon appeared, including several yard switchers. The switchers were un-
necessary (we had no yard) but so inexpensive that having taken
the time and consumed the gas to reach the store, failure to buy
them would have meant we weren't being cost-effective.

We also bought "rolling stock," which meant freight cars and
passenger cars. The locomotives, however, continued to be our
chief objects of veneration, and John's favorite was a Norfolk
and Western steam engine with a nose rounded like a bullet.
This locomotive was thrillingly long; in real life, with tender, it
measured 109 feet. Metal fairings imparted a sleek, streamlined
look. The engine was black, with a Tuscan-red stripe that curved
up from the cowcatcher, then ran back along the side, extending
in an unwavering straight line to the end of the tender.

On one visit to Berkshire Hills, we bought several plastic kits
from which to construct buildings. I began by assembling a sta-

tion and a saloon. Next came a coaling tower and a water tank. I had done well enough with the roadbed and the track laying, and I was quietly pleased with what I supposed was my influence on John. But with the kits, things began to unravel. As a kid, I had built dozens of model boats and cars, always sloppily. I'd never bothered to file off the little nubbins that connected the parts to the sprues, and I'd crease the decals and smear the glue. Now, thirty-five years later, it was just as bad. I didn't know how to get John Allen's weathered effects, and my finished models had a bright, plastic look, like the American Flyer trains.

An explanation was called for. I told John that I had never had my heart in assembling kits because anybody could build a kit, kits weren't *original*. I pointed out that John Allen's buildings weren't kits—they were built from scratch, which explained why he didn't mind lavishing so much time on them.

I felt my point was made, but in making it, I was now committed to finding a source for scratch-built structures. At Berkshire Hills, I had bought a storage barn made by a local modeler from real wood and tin. It was terrific, but when I inquired about buying more, I was told there weren't any.

John was disillusioned by my model building, and I began to wonder how he would feel when he realized that I wouldn't be able to do the wiring. I had been able to hook up the main loop, but the time was coming to confront the switches and the dreaded subject of reverse polarity. With Lionel's three-rail setup, no matter where your engine was on the layout, or what direction it was going, the power always came off the middle (positive) rail and was returned to the outer (negative) rails. With the HO two-rail system, however, the power would come off one rail and return to the other, which was fine until you looped around and tried to come back in the opposite direction, encountering polarity that was now backward. The answer, I had read, was to make the loop into a separate zone, isolating it from the straight so that while the engine was traversing the loop, you had time to reverse the polarity of the straight. Each section required a separate power feed and a pair of toggle switches back at the control panel.

Once I understood how many isolated sections of track, how much wire running hither and yon, and how many toggles our double-loop layout would require, I knew help was needed. Of course, my mother could have handled the wiring, but she was nearly seventy, and somehow I couldn't picture her crawling around under the layout. (I didn't even want to ask; she would probably have insisted on doing it.) So I called an electrician. In due course a capable young man named Paul Roy arrived and in about a week he wired the layout.

After all, a Lionel Dad wasn't expected to bother with stuff like this.

We grouped the plastic buildings to simulate a town, and I cut a piece of the blue foam to suggest the outline of a mountain, placing it behind the buildings. John built three false-front stores out of cardboard. The stores were slightly lopsided, and the doors and windows were just drawn on, but they definitely caught the spirit of the Old West. We had the beginnings of something.

Then John began to have doubts about the Western motif. He began making drawings of other track plans. He was going back to square one, challenging the premise of what we had built so far. For days, he generated track plan after track plan; they appeared on pads, scraps of paper, even in the margins of his textbooks. He seemed on the verge of starting his own layout; we even discussed where it might go.

I tried to stay composed. My role as Dad called for me to encourage him, but if he began another layout, it would be *his* layout, and the existing one would become *my* layout—not *our* layout. I wanted a layout, but I wanted to share it with John. To me, going it alone would mean abandoning the project. Despite the success of his false-front stores, John, now eight, was still three years younger than I had been when I failed with the burlap. I feared that if he attempted his own layout, we would wind up with a basement full of junk.

And then the moment passed. John stopped making his diagrams, and our project was back on track.

Linn Westcott's book on John Allen documented the layout but said little about the techniques used in its construction. In *Scenery for Model Railroads* by Bill McClanahan, I found a how-to book that contained information on Allen's approach as well as tips from other top modelers.

It was easy to have confidence in Bill. He was shown on the cover leaning out over his layout, wearing a striped engineer's cap and smoking a pipe—shades of the Lionel catalog! However, his book's subtitle, *How the Experts Do It Made Easy for Beginners,* was misleading. Turning to the chapter on mountains (contributed by Linn Westcott), I found a lengthy lesson on geology, along with the suggestion that you place a doormat at the exit of the train room so as not to track the mess from the layout up into the house.

Geology! Doormats! This wasn't what I had bought the book for. Next came a long list of tools and materials that I didn't have and special products like HydroCal and Keene's cement, which I had no idea how to get. A bewildering series of steps followed, more intricate than any recipe from a fancy cookbook.

The next chapter I read brought no relief. Offering advice on color and texture, it was dense with formulas and charts. Most sobering of all were step-by-step instructions for creating the rock castings that were essential to achieving the John Allen look. You were to begin by making rubber molds of real rocks, using eight layers of latex, each applied by hand and allowed to dry before the next layer could be started. Then you were to fill the molds with plaster (eleven types were discussed) and press them into place on the scenery base (i.e., the foam blocks), holding the molds absolutely steady until the plaster dried (and here was another chart, for drying times). Each mold yielded a rock no bigger than the size of your fist, and my mind reeled at the prospect of spending the next few months crouched next to the layout, my hand gripping a rubber mold.

The McClanahan book both showed me what to do and convinced me not to do it. What was the appeal of using methods already perfected by others and known to be laborious? (Here, surfacing again, was my rationale for not building kits.) Better to gamble on something new. What if I could find a way to carve the foam itself? I would sidestep the whole onerous business of the molds.

I grabbed a saw and began cutting a piece of foam, shaping it to look like the cross section of a mountainside. Then I made another, and another. I stacked the pieces side by side, like books on a shelf. Each became a template for the next one, but I intentionally made slight changes to the outlines as I went along—a geology of deviation. If a piece didn't look right, I put it aside for later use. When eight or ten were ready, I glued them together. This gave me a block that was light and easy to move around. I cut enough pieces of foam to make three or four more blocks. The Westcott method produced a thin plaster shell, which meant his mountains were hollow and vulnerable to damage. By contrast, a few dents would only add character to our hunks of foam. And our tunnels would be real tunnels, bored through the foam.

Also real was the mess. The static electricity encouraged the small leftover pieces of foam to cling to my clothes and hair. Linn Westcott had recommended a doormat, but what we really needed was an industrial-strength Electrolux.

The lumps of foam, crude as they were, gave the layout a sense of scale that had been missing. But this led us to realize that what we had been dreaming about just wasn't going to fit within the real-life boundaries of the existing platform. No matter how John and I stretched our imaginations, the layout now just seemed like a souped-up version of our original oval on the four-by-eight-foot sheet of plywood, where the trains went around and around. Real trains didn't go around and around—that's what toy trains did. Real trains went to specific places, and came back. The more I thought about this, the more I found myself looking off across the basement to a far-away corner. If the trains went *there,* I thought, they would be making an actual journey. The layout would be at least fifty feet long, and from fifty feet away an HO locomotive is barely visible.

The addition would double the size of the layout—and double the work ahead. But having barely started, and never having finished a layout and therefore not knowing what was actually involved, for me doubling the work was merely an abstraction.

Anyway, I liked what I was doing. And it wasn't as if some grand plan were being violated. Building the extension meant working toward something I now saw as well worth doing. It also meant an immediate return to the comfort zone of plywood,

Homasote, cork, and track laying. Mountain building could once again be postponed. An intriguing aspect of the expansion was that it would make our layout bigger than John Allen's, at least in one dimension. (His was twenty-four by thirty-two feet.) I wanted to call Bill Berry, the carpenter, immediately, and ask him to start the new platform.

John was less enthusiastic. He didn't like that my plans for the extension included just one loop. (I envisioned the track swallowed up in the landscape, in the style of John Allen.) John was as territorial as Cornelius Vanderbilt about the loops. As it had been with the four-by-eight-foot layout, his loop was the inner, mine the outer. The logical choice for the proposed extension was my outer loop, and despite repeated guarantees that his trains would be welcome on my tracks, he refused to endorse the project unless his loop was extended, too. Fearing that he might return to the idea of building his own layout, I quickly gave in.

The day Bill arrived to add to the platform, I was scheduled for my annual physical. Somewhere between the eye test and the weigh-in, the conversation shifted to the train layout, and my doctor, Peter Gott, suggested I meet a man named Don Buckley, whose layout he had just seen. Buckley dealt in fine American antique furniture, but what he really treasured was his layout. When he invited me to visit, I could see why: every detail was perfect. Don held a master's certificate from the National Model Railroad Association, which meant, among many other things, that he was capable of scratch-building structures and even locomotives. I explained that I dreamed of a layout like his but had few of the requisite skills. Don suggested that I get some help and said he knew of someone who might be willing to work with me part-time.

"He can do everything," Don said. The man he had in mind worked part-time at Berkshire Hills, and his name was Rolf

Schneider. Rolf Schneider—I already knew him! He had solved the mystery of the *Maine Central*.

The *Maine Central* was the most expensive locomotive John and I had bought so far, and to our great disappointment it refused to run smoothly; instead, it staggered along like a misfiring car. With our limited experience, all we could do was clean its wheels, which we did with increasing ferocity as our frustration mounted. The engine picked up the current from the wheels of its tender, an arrangement that we guessed might be flawed in some way. We took the locomotive back to Berkshire Hills, where the owner of the store gave it a cursory glance, handed it back, and told us our track probably needed cleaning. We said our other locomotives ran fine. He just shrugged.

Back home, the *Maine Central* still wouldn't run. I was ready to abandon hope, but the engine was beautiful, and John loved it as much as his Norfolk and Western model (which had seized up and was out of commission for good). I knew the right thing to do was to go back to Berkshire Hills and confront the owner. Anticipating failure, I went alone. To my relief, the owner was taking a day off. The man behind the desk was slightly built, bearded, and friendly. He studied the locomotive, turning it in his hands like an archaeologist examining a freshly unearthed artifact. "Well, I see the wheels are clean," he said, smiling. I thought he looked like an elf on leave from the North Pole. He ran the engine on a short piece of test track, watching as it sparked and surged. He pointed to the tender.

"See here?" he said. "The axles are shorting out on the trucks." Fixing it would require axles with plastic bushings, which he apologized for not having in stock. He would order them, but they would take a while to arrive because the manufacturer was new to the business. He suggested I leave the engine with him. A month later, when John and I went to pick it up, this same nice fellow was there again, and that is when we found out that his name was Rolf Schneider. We tried to pay, but he shook his head and said, "No charge."

The morning after my visit to Don Buckley, I talked with Rolf, and he said he would be happy to work with me. We specifically discussed his building a switching yard, which Don Buckley had said no self-respecting layout could do without. It was late February. My racing career had led me into sportscasting, and the season was about to begin, so we agreed that Rolf wouldn't start until after the summer.

I thought that with a helper of Rolf's skill and experience, I could finish the layout in a couple of winters.

Rolf was born in northern Germany in the late stages of World War II. His family lived in Bremen, an industrial city that was a prime target for Allied bombing. In the last weeks of her pregnancy, Rolf's mother moved to the relative safety of the country. Her situation was ironic because she was an American, and the bombs she was dodging were ours.

When the war was over, Rolf's grandfather, who was an engineer at a trolley company, built him a tricycle out of old trolley parts. Riding around the yards, bumping over rails, Rolf fell in love with trains. Meanwhile his father, a barber, was unable to find work, and he brought his family to the United States. It was 1949, and they settled in Brooklyn. For his first Christmas in America, Rolf was given a set of Lionel trains. Describing the Lionel equipment as "too toylike," he soon switched to HO and built himself a layout on the ubiquitous sheet of four-by-eight-foot plywood.

After two years of college, he went to work as an architectural model maker. Then a coincidence occurred that was to shape his life. Through an architect he met at work, he was introduced to a man who had just started a layout and needed help. He offered to employ Rolf full-time, and Rolf took the job.

Another layout job followed, in Canaan, Connecticut, where Rolf met a local resident named Dave Townsend, who was also building a layout. Dave and Rolf quickly became friends and decided to open a hobby shop.

Unfortunately, business was slow, and the partners decided to sell out. Rolf returned to New York to build models for the Port Authority, a job that ended abruptly when the model department was closed. Soon Rolf found himself back in Canaan. He leased space in the back of the hobby shop from its new owner, intending to support himself by building models for the area's architects. When that didn't work out, he began working part-time at the shop, which is how John and I met him.

As fall approached, I grew apprehensive about having Rolf work with me. So far, John and I had made all the decisions about the layout, and it was ours in a way that was special to both of us. Now, presumably, Rolf and I would be deciding things, and I worried that John would feel left out. I also wondered what it would be like to work so closely with another adult. In the studio, Ellen and I had our own rooms, separated by a hallway, and I was used to working by myself. Would Rolf and I get in each other's way? Would he bring a radio or distract me by wanting to talk? It turned out these fears were groundless. Rolf was as anxious to get on with the job as I was. In any case, I was so preoccupied by whatever I was doing, I barely noticed what he was up to.

Which was a lot. Rolf never seemed to be hurrying, but at the end of the day he had always accomplished more than I would have thought possible. His experience led him to propose solutions to problems I hadn't even realized we had. It was quickly agreed that his role would be expanded beyond building the yard; he would do the wiring for the layout's new section, ballast the tracks, build the structures—in short, he would do everything except build the scenery.

Rolf had his own tools, which he brought with him each day in a carpenter's toolbox. The tools were scaled to the job; his saw, for example, had such fine teeth that you could run your finger over the blade without cutting yourself. He had tiny files, knives, pliers, and clamps. He also owned some relatively expensive equipment, miniature power tools specially designed by Dremel for model making. But his finest tools were his hands. When a model was partially assembled, he was able to hold half a dozen parts together and still somehow have a hand free for gluing.

Rolf's plans for the yard included a roundhouse, a working turntable, a coaling tower, a water tower, and an assortment of maintenance shacks. These were things I couldn't even begin to think of building myself. For Rolf, however, all this was "no problem," a phrase I was beginning to realize he applied to virtually everything.

To make room for the yard, we needed to widen the platform at the left end. This meant another visit from our project carpenter, Bill Berry, and we took full advantage of the opportunity by asking him to add some storage cabinets, install a sink, and build a desk for Rolf. The desk was particularly important to me because I realized how much I wanted Rolf to feel at home in our basement. His first project, as he waited for supplies to arrive for the yard, was a viaduct that looked every bit as good as anything on John Allen's layout, and I could already see that Rolf Schneider was going to loom large in my future.

Before he left, Bill installed a drawer next to what we were calling Judy's Loop. This drawer contained her power pack and allowed her to be right next to her trains when she ran them. This apparently thoughtful gesture grew out of fear of Judy getting anywhere near the main control panel. She was almost four, and while I occasionally indulged myself with the faint hope she might defy tradition and show a true interest in trains, John and I were both unsettled by her style of operation. Wearing a yellow bathrobe and standing on a box that allowed her to see out over the layout, Judy distilled the broad spectrum of the way trains could run into a single idea: the crash.

Christmas approached and, recalling my childhood joy at discovering a new Lionel locomotive under the tree, I decided to buy John an engine that would top even the *Maine Central,* which, thanks to Rolf, was now running smoothly. But nothing at Berkshire Hills was up to the task. I saw my chance when we drove to New York so that the kids could go skating at Rockefeller Center. Leaving Ellen at the rink with John and Judy, and promising that I would return in under an hour, I hurried south along Fifth Avenue looking for a hobby store called the Red Caboose.

The Red Caboose, as its name suggests, specialized in trains, especially HO trains. I had a vague recollection of the place dating from a visit years before, and I had foolishly neglected to check the address. I remembered the store as being several floors up, in the middle of a block near the midtown diamond district. A few minutes brought me in range, and I started walking down each street, peering through the clutter of signs and lights. It was cold and dark; the sidewalks were icy and crowded with holiday shoppers. I started to run, darting down block after block, until suddenly I knew I had gone too far. The Red Caboose was somewhere behind me, not ahead. By the time I found it, half an hour was gone.

It was about ninety degrees in the store, but I couldn't squander a moment trying to find a place to hang my parka. Narrow aisles were separated by shelving that extended from floor to ceiling and bulged with specialized items that only the most advanced modeler would need or even know existed. The customers were divided into two camps. The veterans appeared to live in the store; they had their coats off and were poking through the shelves, affecting a stylized indifference to the holiday pressures—they were long past the stage where model railroading had anything to do with Christmas. The rest of us were rookies. We crowded around the locomotive case, jockeying for position.

"Mister?" The salesman was staring at me through thick, grimy glasses. I had barely begun to inspect what must have been at least one hundred locomotives. But the salesman was impatient, and I knew if I didn't make my choice fast I wouldn't be getting another chance soon. Numbly, I pointed to an engine that was at least *longer* than any we owned.

Moments later, I had left the crowd at the case and was standing in the back of a long line at the cash register. I clasped the new engine wheels-up, trying to avoid seeing how ordinary it was. I took a furtive glance—there, my fears were confirmed. The proportions were all wrong, and one of the decals was crooked. My mind raced. I imagined Christmas morning, the tree, the cheery fire, the array of presents—and John reaching for the long, heavy package he would know instinctively was his Main Present. . . .

I hadn't even seen it run; the salesman said the test track had shorted out—a cynical lie, I assumed, no doubt intended to keep things moving. I knew I should not buy this engine. But my time had run out and I couldn't deal with the idea of leaving the Red Caboose empty-handed.

The line was at a dead stop: a customer was arguing with the cashier. Looking for distraction, I reached for a book on a nearby shelf. It was a random selection, but as I leafed through it I became enthralled by superb pictures of frontier Colorado and a rugged-looking railroad I had never heard of: the Colorado Midland.

When my turn finally came to pay, I held out the locomotive and the book.

"That's very rare," the cashier said, nodding at the book. "It'll cost you two hundred dollars." Stunned, I quickly returned it to the shelf. Two hundred dollars! Even the locomotive was only $125.

That night, when I was describing my sortie to Ellen, I said that what was so frustrating was that I had caught glimpses, in that book, of exactly what I now realized I wanted our railroad to look like.

"What was it called?" she asked.

On Christmas Day, I unwrapped one of the best Christmas presents of my life, *The Colorado Midland*. It had been written by a Colorado historian named Morris Cafky, and the principal photography was by William Henry Jackson, whose work I had already come to admire.

I soon acquired a companion book, Dan Abbott's *Colorado Midland Railway*. These two volumes were to create a looking glass through which I could step from our basement into a world of granite and iron that had existed one hundred years before.

As for the locomotive, it was every bit the dud I had feared. It derailed at every switch and was soon relegated to an upper shelf in the cabinet, where it remains to this day.

JOHN JAMES HAGERMAN

The measurement from the inside edge of one rail across to the inside edge of the other is defined as the gauge. The various gauges chosen by the early railroads were determined by local conditions and cost. Wider gauges offered more stability and a better ride, but they required more of everything: bigger roadbeds, tunnels, and bridges, plus larger locomotives and cars.

Different gauges worked fine until railroads grew large enough to interconnect with one another. Then the freight and passengers being hauled would have to be transferred when their train reached the end of the line. To avoid this waste of time and money, most of Europe settled on a common gauge. Measuring four feet, eight and one half inches, it became known as "standard gauge." Standard gauge got an early foothold in the United States, too, and any serious thoughts about other gauges vanished in 1862 when President Lincoln stipulated standard gauge for the Transcontinental Railroad.

Railroading in the mountains, however, had its own rules. The great designer of mountain railroads was a man named Otto Mears, and he was faced with trying to find a way to put down tracks in places so remote that even the surveyors had trouble reaching them. Mears and the other mountain railway designers used a narrow gauge (three feet) and small, light, locomotives and cars. The curves could be tight (allowing trains to zigzag up steep slopes), the trestles fragile, and the tunnels narrow. The small trains picked their way over the crude roadbeds like mountain goats, usually not going much over 20 mph.

John and I liked the homemade look of narrow gauge, which served the remote mining towns that we envisioned building on our layout. But our HO tracks were standard gauge. Since it was too late for us to change, we were intrigued when we noticed—on Christmas Day, as we leafed through my new book—that the Colorado Midland was also standard gauge.

The Midland had been conceived in the 1880s, when standard gauge fever was running high in the rapidly growing town of Colorado Springs, eighty miles south of Denver. Almost fifteen years had passed since the completion of the Transcontinental Railroad, which ran through Wyoming and northern Utah, and forward-thinking citizens of Colorado were aware that if a standard gauge line wasn't built through their state soon, they would forfeit fortunes in trade and tourism.

A route heading west from Denver made the most sense topographically, but near Colorado Springs, a break in the front wall of the Rockies called Ute Pass offered a reasonable alternative. The citizens of Colorado Springs were full of pride and ambition, and they included a recent arrival named James John

Hagerman. Hagerman was a Milwaukee businessman who had moved west to recover from tuberculosis. He had made millions in mining, mostly in Michigan's Upper Peninsula, and after the altitude and salubrious airs of Colorado Springs had put him back on his feet, he plunged into the mining business once again. He acquired large holdings in Aspen and Leadville, towns that in those days were nearly inaccessible. To get his ore out of the mountains, Hagerman needed a railroad, and the proponents of standard gauge successfully appealed to his ego. Doing things big was Hagerman's style.

Work on the Midland began in 1886. Heading west from Colorado Springs, the line climbed from six thousand feet to more than nine thousand feet in the first twenty-seven miles. Grades were as steep as 4 percent, which was the upper limit for standard gauge. The finished route writhed for 224 miles through varied terrain, which Jackson's photographs in the Morris Cafky book show to be consistently spectacular.

Scale changes were dizzying: immense boulders and rock outcroppings dwarfed the locomotives and cars. Broad vistas made telegraph poles appear no bigger than toothpicks. Place-names were undomesticated: Hell Gate, Idlewild, Wild Horse, Ironclad Hills. The surveys called for seventeen tunnels, including four in a single half-mile stretch. Long sections of roadbed were chiseled into nearly vertical cliffs. Ravines were spanned by cutting down thousands of trees, which were then used to build dense wooden trestles.

To the modern eye, the men who built the Midland raped the land. But they can't have seen it that way at the time; photograph after photograph shows their innocent pride. Here was a shot of a team of bearded carpenters posing by their handiwork, the timbered arch of a tunnel portal. Here was an engineer dressed in his Sunday best standing with his wife and young child in front of his freshly polished locomotive. In the late 1880s, the Midland's route offered the grandeur of man challenging nature, at a time when this was still a fair fight. It was a route through the clouds, across an inspiring landscape that could have been painted by Thomas Moran or Frederick Church, and the men who built it were seen as authentic heroes, strong and skillful, men an emerging civilization could rely upon.

The Midland's signature was a seven-mile-long section called the High Line, in the Saguache Range. To the east was Leadville, a mining town oozing with the Old West character that John and I wanted to re-create. The High Line crossed such mountainous terrain that the equipment and material to build it had to be hauled in by burros. With most of the supplies consumed by the railroad, little was left over for housing, and the track gangs resorted to living in sod huts and even caves.

The High Line's tracks twisted back and forth across a valley, steadily gaining altitude. Near the top, the surveyors ran out of options, and the engineers came to the rescue by designing an immense wooden trestle a quarter of a mile long and eighty-five feet high. It carried the rails soaring out above a valley, then curved through 90 degrees before rejoining the grade. After five more turns, the line reached its maximum elevation—11,500 feet—and entered a two-thousand-foot-long tunnel that bored under the Continental Divide.

Extravagant engineering like this was typical of the late nineteenth century. It was an expression of confidence, the belief that a man—in this case James John Hagerman—could do anything. His name was stamped everywhere on diagrams of the High Line: the big trestle was Hagerman Trestle, a nearby lake was Hagerman Lake, the tunnel was the Hagerman Tunnel.

The railroad was completed in November 1890, and the rigors of construction were immediately replaced by a new struggle:

keeping the line running. The moment winter arrived, train crews found themselves battling wind and drifting snow on a scale the Midland's designers had never imagined. Rotary snow-plows were purchased and snowsheds constructed, but these measures were no match for the conditions.

The Midland's problems with weather had become public knowledge even while track was still being laid. Smelling blood, a group of investors formed a company and boldly began drilling a two-mile-long tunnel two thousand feet *directly below* the Mid-land's existing Hagerman Tunnel. The new tunnel, called the Busk-Ivanhoe, was a shortcut that eliminated most of the High Line, including all the valley switchbacks and the huge trestle. It was an engineering triumph—although twenty men were killed building it, mostly by explosives that detonated prematurely.

The Midland began renting the Busk-Ivanhoe tunnel the day it was finished. The group of investors who financed it did not include Hagerman or any of the other Midland owners, and from the beginning they charged usurious fees. Hagerman was reeling from the cost of building his railroad (nearly four times what had originally been projected), and the profits that should have been bailing him out were going into the pockets of the Busk-Ivanhoe investors.

Despite the constant tension between the two camps, the Midland continued to rent the tunnel for almost four years, until October 1897, when yet another rate hike so infuriated the rail-road's executives that they decided to call the tunnel company's bluff. Negotiations went nowhere, and by the time the contract expired the Midland's managers had renovated the High Line. Trains once again clawed their way up the valley switchbacks. The first winter back was mild, but in January 1899, the weather turned bad.

When the first storm hit, a cattle train was trapped by a col-

lapsed snowshed and the cattle all froze to death. Before the car-
casses could be removed, a second storm pummeled the line. To
clear the tracks, four or five locomotives were coupled together
with a plow at the front, and they would attempt to batter their
way through the drifts. The plow was something out of a
Leonardo da Vinci sketchbook of war machines: a boxcar with a
giant, multibladed fan grafted on one end. The whirling blades
ingested the snow, then hurled it off to the side of the tracks.
Photographs by the indefatigable Jackson show the snow arcing
into the air, a plume of white silhouetted against the black smoke
that billowed up from the engines. But some drifts were as high
as the tops of the locomotive's cabs, traction on the slippery rails
was poor, and the plows would bog down. In desperation, the
Midland arranged to borrow a different kind of plow from the
Santa Fe. Called a Jull, it was a huge auger designed to literally
screw its way through the snow. The Jull had worked for the
Santa Fe, but in the Midland's hands it soon encountered a drift
that was thick with ice and it jammed, its gears stripped.

The crews often had no choice but to clear the tracks by hand,
shoveling their way through snowbanks twenty feet high. Ice
froze the switches and had to be cut away with axes. Locomotives derailed. More snowsheds collapsed. Whenever the men
managed to clear a few miles of the line, another storm would
sweep in. Coal ran out, so the trainmen stoked their fireboxes
with wood from trees they chopped down along the tracks. They
melted snow to provide water for the boilers. When the engines
broke down, replacement parts—if any could be found—were
lashed to toboggans, which men then hauled to the stricken
trains.

It was seventy-seven days before the line was cleared.

Sitting comfortably in my bed at night, reading the Cafky book, I remembered that my friend John Whitman once told me I should have lived in the nineteenth century. Setting aside the hardship of life in those times, I just liked the way things looked then, particularly out west. And here was a book full of pictures that were quintessentially Western. Which features to include in our layout? I wanted them all.

As Rolf began designing the yard, he realized that the Midland's yard in Basalt was a perfect fit. I looked hard at the photographs, closed my eyes, then opened them to see a ghost image superimposed on our bare plywood. The configuration of the tracks, the placement of the yard in relationship to the scenery— it all worked. The Midland's yard even had a mountain exactly where we had a mountain.

The yard was only the beginning. Picture after picture suggested subjects for various spots along the layout. Here was a great place for the Midland's curving steel bridge at Manitou Iron Works. Here was a mine, a marble quarry, a high wooden trestle, a station all waiting to be reborn on our layout. It was eerie, as if we had been building the Midland all along, without knowing it. For a heady moment, I even thought we had *discovered* the Midland, at least as far as model railroading was concerned. But then I happened to be looking again at John Allen's layout and noticed he had given one of his towns the unusual name of Divide. Well, there was a Divide on the Midland route, and as I looked closer at Allen's layout I began to see a dozen landscape elements that only the Midland could have inspired. Allen had (as with everything else) been there first. But instead of being disappointed, I thought we might be doing something right.

It hadn't occurred to me to base our layout on a particular railroad. I had supposed that John and I would eventually invent one. As for a name, I had winced at Allen's Gorre and Daphetid and laughed at others such as the Broak and Kantifordit, the Rare and Tugo, and the Hither, Thither, and Yawn. Calling ours, simply, the Colorado Midland avoided all that.

Adopting the Midland provided a basis for many of the decisions we would have to make along the way. Instead of modeling generic Western topography, it gave us a specific area, south-central Colorado, and a time, 1900, which would guide us in details as diverse as what clothes the figures would wear and what bridge types would be appropriate. Also, the Midland shared some of its line (the part that ran along the Colorado River) with a competing railroad, the Denver & Rio Grande; if John wanted his own railroad, there it was.

The decision to model the Midland also resolved what our trains would look like. The Midland's engines and rolling stock were, to my eyes, fantastic. Their early locomotives, steamers built by the Schenectady Locomotive Works, reminded me of the Eiffel Tower (under construction at the same time) in that they were 95 percent Industrial Revolution, with a few ornate details thrown in to satisfy Victorian sensibilities. They had spare, cylindrical boilers that ended abruptly with squared-off wooden cabs, which were elegantly paneled and sported brass grab rails. The steam dome and the sand dome, both banded in brass, perched on the boiler like bowler hats, and the bell was suspended from a fanciful Baroque bracket. At the front, the iron cowcatchers were sharply pointed and aggressive while the overscale, oil-fired headlamps looked like lanterns borrowed from an old carriage. The passenger cars were finished in mahogany and English oak; the rattan seats reclined and the double-width windows had arched tops. The cabooses were even more exotic: they had cupolas whose roofs curved up at the eaves, like a pagoda's.

The Midland had a charm unusual for railroads of the day. Employees got along with one another and were treated with respect by the management. They became known as the "Midland family." Every spring, excursion trains chugged into the countryside pulling open gondola cars fitted with rows of wooden seats. For a dollar you could spend the day taking in the scenery and picking wildflowers, including primrose, saffron, penstemon, and columbine. The trips were commemorated by photographs that show as many as two hundred women and children posed around, and on, the locomotive. In one shot, the biggest bouquet is in the clutches of the conductor himself. Crews were encouraged to customize their locomotives, and a popular embellishment was a set of antlers attached to the headlamp. In 1905, the Midland carried President Theodore Roosevelt on a hunting trip, and his engine and tender were gaily decorated with flags and bunting.

While much of the Midland's route was rocky and grim, parts of it were rich with spots of idyllic beauty: high mountain plateaus, secret valleys, stands of towering lodgepole pines, and a lovely winding stretch along the banks of the fast-flowing Frying Pan River. In addition to these natural wonders, the route passed architectural confections typical of the day. In Cascade, a summer resort hotel was capped by a Byzantine dome, and in Green Mountain Falls, trains were framed by a gazebo and reflected in a mirrored lake.

In short, the Midland had everything.

As Rolf began to translate the photograph of the Basalt yard into model form, we elected to expand the Midland's engine house, which, like John Allen's, was a simple, two-stall structure, into a four-stall roundhouse complete with turntable. The picture also showed a station and a hotel; we made them the heart of a small town just beyond the yard.

The hotel was actually called the "eating house," thanks to a large dining room on the ground floor. The Midland built several of these eating houses because the route through the mountains was so twisting and steep that no food could be served—or eaten—aboard the trains. The passengers would disembark and rush from the train to the dining room, where long tables were already set with food. Meanwhile, the engine crew would be hurrying to replenish the tender with coal and water, and the moment they were finished (the job took about fifteen minutes), the engineer would blow the whistle, signaling the diners to dash back to the train. Passengers who lingered over a last bite were obliged to wait for the next train in spartan conditions: the upper floors of the eating houses had bare rooms furnished only with cots.

Once our eating house was built, we followed it with a bank, a carriage house, and a grocery store. We also based these on real buildings, and I studied each structure in detail before reducing its dimensions to HO scale. I was surprised to find that buildings that were technically correct often looked too big; I could only fit two or three where my instinct told me I wanted to jam in four or five. I was learning that the optics of the layout allowed for— and actually required—more of everything than you would find in real life. Modelers had a word for this: compression. Compression was the art of fitting big dreams into modest spaces.

After the drawings came matte board models, which we placed on the layout to see how they related to existing structures nearby. When a building passed the test, Rolf would order materials for a finished version. We could buy windows, doors, chimneys, railings, porch posts, and gable vents in various sizes and styles. Siding came in eight-by-ten-inch styrene sheets; you could choose brick, clapboard, board and batten, or stone. Individual strips of wood were also available for corner boards and window casings. Because Rolf was working at Berkshire Hills, we rarely had to wait for anything. He either had what we needed at the shop or, as a dealer, he was able to get it overnight from Walthers, a Milwaukee company that carried a seemingly limitless stock of HO supplies.

Rolf was well along with his work on the yard when Gerry Bill, a friend I had met through racing, arrived. His car was loaded with HO equipment he said he wanted to dispose of before he moved to California. Could I use any of it? I looked through box after box. Gerry's structures, most of them assembled from kits, were an eclectic mix, mostly contemporary, although he had a few Old West buildings, too. Just a few weeks before, this stuff might easily have decided the entire character of our layout, but since we had become bewitched by the Midland, I had to tell him that I thought very few of his things would work out. He said to keep them anyway.

As Rolf began turning out finished structures for the yard, I knew it was time to complete some landscape to go with them. Just a page away from the photo of the Basalt yard was a panorama of a quarry, with the odd name of Peach Blow. Peach Blow was on the Frying Pan River, and behind it was a cliff with an abstract simplicity that suggested an uneven row of books, with a talus slope at the base.

I studied Peach Blow and became convinced that here was a rock formation that lent itself to being modeled in blue foam. The architect Louis Kahn once famously posed the question, "Brick, what do you want to be?" The manufacturers of the blue foam, Dow Chemical, had designed it to be used in sheets, as insulation; that, presumably, was what it most "wanted" to be. I was about to find out if perhaps it might also like being cut up and turned into the Rockies.

I collected my tools. A marking pen. The small handsaw I had already used to rough out the mountain forms that I had glued into blocks. A rasp. A chisel. A few sheets of coarse sandpaper. Four tubes of adhesive to be applied to the foam using a metal device that resembled a pistol. It was a motley assortment, but definitely in the spirit of a hobby that espoused the use of everyday tools and materials.

Laying the track had called for a continuous stream of precise measurements, but I sculpted the cliffs entirely by eye, trying to translate what I saw in the photograph into three dimensions. Each piece of foam was two inches thick, so I began with a modular approach, making the width of the individual outcroppings either one, two, or three pieces wide. Once the basic shapes were established, I chamfered the edges, gouged holes, and generally roughed them up. With no directions to follow, every step was a guess added on top of other guesses. Rolf kept his distance, tactfully detouring around the growing mess. At the end of the day, I had a three-foot stretch of blue cliffs.

I pulled a chair over to the edge of the layout. In college, I had majored in painting, and I continued to paint during my racing years. I had experienced many moments when an image suddenly went from looking tentative and incomplete to taking on a life of its own, with a clear identity. Now, in one day, I had gone from my lumps of foam to the cliffs at Peach Blow.

In the next few weeks, I spent up to twelve hours a day on the layout, seven days a week, and the last thing I did before falling asleep was to look through the Midland book for ideas for the next day. In one sense, this was hard work; however, in the absence of the tension that usually goes with a real job, it hardly seemed like work at all. I was used to tension and at times I had even welcomed it, assuming it was a necessary ingredient if I was to perform at my best. But tension brings its own distractions, and now I was surprised to see how much work I was getting done, day after day, without it.

The progress, however, was only relative. When I looked out across the bare platform and thought about the time I had spent already, barely making a dent in the project, it was easy for me to get discouraged. So I made another uncharacteristic decision: I decided not to worry about it. After all, I told myself, I was just playing with trains.

It was odd to be in the house, yet virtually estranged from family life. I could easily tell what was going on just by listening to the footsteps above. Judy would be the first to come home, her arrival triggering a familiar sequence of sounds, most of them loud. The front door would slam, and then I'd hear clomping as she went to the closet and took off her boots. *Thunk*—her backpack would hit the floor. Next she would leap around the living room, which was directly above the layout; dust particles would shake loose and float down onto my head. Finally she would appear at the top of the basement stairs, wearing her overalls and holding a Popsicle. Judy's idea of visiting the layout was to leave things different than they were when she arrived. A locomotive that had been parked in the yard might find itself at the bottom of a ravine. A stuffed animal might appear in the mountains. Chunks of blue foam that had been swept into a neat pile might find themselves widely dispersed. Surfaces became sticky.

When John visited, he showed keen interest in our progress, nodding appreciatively when he was shown the recent work. He always had a perceptive comment, and a compliment. But he had

homework to do, and he rarely stayed long. I sensed he understood that the direction of the layout was now in Rolf's hands
and mine—not his. If he didn't like it, he didn't say anything to
me, and I was so absorbed with what I was doing that I just
bulled ahead.

As the weeks passed, Rolf's unfailing good humor seemed to
seep through into the structures he was building. They were res-
olutely crisp and clean, with a freshly minted look that hardly
seemed in character for a town inspired by Leadville. I thought
they should show some wear and tear, and I urged him to "Skuz
it up!" But Rolf was congenitally incapable of skuzzing anything
up, especially a pristine building he had just assembled. Finally
he managed to paint some rusty streaks on a tin roof, an effect
that was so successful that I began specifying tin roofs for everything. I thought Rolf had achieved a breakthrough.

Then one day I glanced up to see him installing a bright green
lawn. Now, thanks to the Cafky book, the Colorado of my
mind's eye existed in shades of gray, and the grimmer things
could be made to look, the better. But Rolf was so happy with his
lawn he was actually *humming*. What to do?

"Rolf . . ."

"Um?"

"I love the lawn." Pause. "I—I'm just not absolutely sure it's
exactly right for, you know, the *feeling* I sort of thought we were
going for here, if you know what I mean. I kinda think of these
places as, well, ah, struggling *outposts,* grimy with soot and—"

"Yes!" Rolf was beaming in agreement. "I think of them that
way, too. That's why I thought we had better cheer things up."

But soon he stopped work on the lawn and became a reluctant master of rusticity, turning out ramshackle picket fences,
tottering outhouses, and a bridge that he assured me was of a
type abandoned by the Midland because of its history of struc-

tural failures. He was really hitting his stride when it came to building a bottling plant for Newman's Own.

Newman's Own was, so far, our only industry, and it offered an opportunity to bring an anecdotal element to the layout. I had met Paul Newman through racing, and Ellen was designing the labels for his fledgling food company. The company was giving all its profits to charity and was so impeccably good that it gave me no choice: our Newman's Own would have to be irredeemably bad.

We located the factory where it could do the most harm: on the banks of a mountain stream, whose crystal clear water it polluted with sewage and industrial waste. On the loading dock, the shipping crates were empty and workers dozed, surrounded by empty beer bottles. Meanwhile, a Ping-Pong game was going on at a table Rolf had fitted with a net fashioned from a sliver of toilet paper—and one of the players looked suspiciously like Newman himself.

THIN AIR

By the time Rolf completed Newman's Own, the yard and most of the town's other buildings were finished, too. At Rolf's suggestion, we named the town Cielo Vista, after the street on which John Allen had lived.

As Rolf built the town, I modeled the bluffs that rose up nearly vertically behind it, using the blue foam and adding some highly detailed polyurethane rocks made by a company called Mountains in Minutes. Sealing the foam, which was porous and absorbed ordinary paint like a sponge, called for a thick latex paint that had been developed to give surfaces a stuccolike effect. The paint transformed the foam into a white mass that looked as if it had been carved out of a solid block of marble.

I assumed the next steps—adding color, then texture—would be easy, and for a moment I found myself wondering if our layout, when it was finished, might actually be competitive with John Allen's. Then I realized we still didn't have a single Colorado Midland locomotive or any Midland rolling stock. We had no trees, bushes, or figures. No part of the layout, however small, was truly finished. We were a long way from competing with anyone.

Nevertheless, the more I studied John Allen's layout, the more I came to think that the individual elements were not all as awesome as I had first believed. For example, some of his structures were clumsy, much of his rock work was crude, and parts of the backdrop had been painted unconvincingly. None of this mattered, of course, because the total effect was far greater than the sum of the parts, but it did underscore how much of the Gorre and Daphetid's magic was due to Allen's artistic vision rather than to his specific modeling skills.

Allen had put this vision to good use when he photographed his layout. In shot after shot, he used it like a stage set, leveraging the modeling itself to create specific moods. His technical skill was complemented by a fine sense of composition and an instinct for narrative. The legend of the layout survived the fire because the reality was in the pictures as much as what had existed in John Allen's basement.

As my appreciation of his photography grew, so did my interest in taking some pictures of our layout, even in its unfinished state. One day, I got out our camera and shot a couple of rolls. I was excited by what I saw through the lens, but the developed images managed to be both yellowish and dark at the same time. Most of the subject matter was out of focus, and the locomotives looked formless and black, like lumps of coal.

Rolf suggested I get help from his friends Steve and Tony,

who ran a camera store called Snap Shop. I took some more pictures, and they spread the prints on the counter and talked me through what was wrong. Every Friday for the next few weeks, I took my film to Snap Shop, had it critiqued, and left the store with whatever new equipment Steve and Tony thought I needed to get to the next level. Special blue lights solved the yellowish cast. Using a tripod made longer exposures possible, which increased the depth of field and eliminated the blurring. Shining light on the locomotive with a flashlight sharpened details.

"*Model Railroader* will kill for these," I told John, kidding him about our bet. But I was learning all over again just how good John Allen really was.

Ellen and I painted the white cliffs using thin acrylic washes applied in layers. They looked convincing, but I realized that what they evoked wasn't the granite landscape of the Midland route. It was more southwestern Colorado, more the soft tans and umbers of the Uncompahgre Plateau's scoured sandstone. My landscape was full of eroded buttes and pinnacles, cracks and fractures. I had drawn my inspiration from the cliffs at the Peach Blow quarry, and I now saw this had been a geological anomaly, a chunk of southwestern Colorado that had turned up about 150 miles northeast of where it was supposed to be. But I was too pleased with what I had to consider starting over. Better, I thought, to relocate the Midland.

The Midland's earnings had sagged due to the blizzards of 1899, but it was worse for the Busk-Ivanhoe tunnel company, which suffered the expenses of maintenance without seeing any income at all. In May, the Midland made an offer to purchase the tunnel. It was accepted, and the High Line was closed for good. At last, the Midland began to make money, and one good year followed another for almost a decade. Competition with the Denver & Rio Grande was brisk, but people were flocking to Colorado, creating enough business to allow both lines to thrive. The mines in Leadville and Aspen were coughing up ore as if the entire earth was made of the stuff. In addition to the ore, trains hauled coke, coal, and steadily increasing quantities of cattle.

By 1908, however, the Denver & Rio Grande had upgraded to standard gauge. For their new tracks, they bought locomotives that were more powerful than the Midland's. With these engines, and a less mountainous (although slightly longer) route, they could pull more cars per train and run faster. Their business increased, eroding the Midland's market share at a time when the market itself was beginning to shrink. Automobiles were arriving in Colorado by the thousands, cutting into the passenger traffic of both lines.

By 1914, as World War I was breaking out in Europe, the Midland had started a long slide into debt. In the spring of 1917, foreclosure proceedings began. The auction of the Midland's assets was set for April 21. America had entered the war two weeks before, and the auction was attended by junk dealers intending to buy the railroad for its value as scrap iron. But just as the Midland was going on the block, a Colorado Springs businessman named Albert E. Carlton drove up and, amid much drama, outbid the junk dealers. He paid $1,425,000.

Locals saw Carlton's purchase of the Midland as a largely philanthropic gesture, but in fact he controlled a widespread network of industries and banks, and ownership of the railroad dovetailed with his interests in a number of ways. Unhappily for Carlton, however, events were to keep him from running his railroad as he might have planned.

American involvement in the war was increasing, and the

movement of troops and equipment began to clog the country's railroads. In late December, the federal government created the United States Railroad Administration, whose purpose was to centralize control and clear things up. As USRA officials studied maps back in Washington, they assigned the Midland extra business purely because it took a more direct route through the Rockies than the Denver & Rio Grande. But the bonanza was to be short-lived. The additional traffic, so welcome at first, exposed the Midland's Achilles' heel. Twenty-seven years before, James John Hagerman had gloried in a route that tackled terrain tougher than any standard gauge line had ever traversed before, and now the struggle to get ever longer trains over the steep grades called for more powerful locomotives, which Carlton could not afford. In May 1918, the USRA realized that the railroad had become a bottleneck and decreed that *all* traffic in the area be diverted to the Denver & Rio Grande.

Carlton stormed to Washington, but when he arrived his protests fell on deaf ears. Overnight, the Midland went from having too much business to having none at all. The entire line was shut down. Locomotives that had pounded over the passes one day sat in the yards the next, their boiler fires extinguished.

Carlton hoped to resume operations when the war was over, and he managed to fight off a court order to tear up the rails. The armistice was signed in mid-November 1918, but the USRA remained in control of the railroads and continued to dictate the assignment of traffic. Carlton was told that the only way the Midland would be allowed to operate was as a division of an existing railroad. He shopped around, but no buyers could be found, and crews began dismantling the line in July 1921. The Midland, up until then, was the largest railroad to have failed in the United States. Its relatively short life—about three decades—suggests that the Midland was ill conceived, tailored too specifically to Hagerman's mining needs. In a sense, it was a toy, James John Hagerman's toy.

A model train layout, in 1:1 scale.

I began to wonder: Could the Midland have been saved? As it happened, when Carlton was casting about for someone to buy the railroad, the Santa Fe's management had actually considered it; they saw the Midland as a potential feeder line for their much larger system, a way to reap profits from Colorado's mining and cattle interests. But they would have had to lay new tracks to connect the two lines.

The Midland's western terminus was at Grand Junction, on the Utah border. Starting there, the Midland would have gone almost due south, along Colorado's western border. The line would have intersected the Dolores River and been able to follow its winding path, encountering towns whose names had the distinctive Midland character: Paradox, Bedrock, Cahone, and Yellow Jacket. It would have crossed Disappointment Creek, with the western edge of the Uncompahgre Plateau as a backdrop. Leaving Colorado at the Four Corners, the extension would have continued south into Arizona, connecting there with the Santa Fe. This part of western Colorado was the landscape our layout most resembled—in fact, one big chunk had been modeled directly on the Uncompahgre Plateau.

Why not imagine that our layout was the extension that saved the Midland? Everything fit, and when I consulted with Rolf and John they said, "Let's do it!" Now we would have features inspired by the real Midland and a fictitious route that might have been its salvation—a promising hybrid that combined the historical prototype with a landscape I was free to invent, uninhibited by claims of reality. Our Colorado Midland would be its own myth.

A model railroad is an object. But, like a play, it has a plot. I felt now that I knew for the first time exactly what was going on in my landscape. I looked with fresh eyes at what we had built so far—my unfinished mountains and backdrop, and Rolf's buildings, which by contrast were detailed down to the last brick and shingle. This strange effect was heightened by the total absence of trees and shrubs; every surface on the layout was hard and smooth. The impression was of a long-deserted colony on the moon, a place without air to breathe. It seemed as if time itself had yet to begin.

The moment had come to start the clock. First, I installed model trees, then bushes. The bushes, which were just small scraps of lichen, linked the buildings to one another. I scattered bits of gravel, which transformed plywood into ground. I brushed a thin, black wash onto the rocks and cliffs, then wiped most of it away, leaving black only in the cracks and crevices. The rocks suddenly had shadows, as if the sun had just come out. Then I tackled the backdrop, painting some faraway mountains and an intense blue sky. Air! Rolf hitched a horse to a post in front of the carriage house, seated an old lady in a rocking chair on the eating house porch, and created a group of twenty or so people having their picture taken as they waited on the platform. When the train pulled in, that was the signal that life on our layout had begun.

Meanwhile, spring had arrived in Sharon. This meant I would be spending the next few months designing houses and covering races for television. I looked forward to that, but it was tough to wrench myself away from the layout. Seeing the finished areas was addictive: I wanted more.

In the fall, a business trip to Colorado gave me an opportunity to see firsthand the landscape we were modeling. I had been in western Colorado two years before, with my family, and we had ridden the narrow gauge tourist railway from Durango north to Silverton and back. This was before our discovery of the Midland, but John and I had already known we wanted our layout's scenery to resemble Colorado, and we spent the entire six-hour ride checking out everything from mountain vistas to the cinders that comprised the ballast. Lunging back and forth across the train, colliding with other passengers and each other, we shot roll after roll as we documented anything that could be even remotely useful for reference when we got back home. Embarrassed to be seen with us, Ellen and Judy withdrew to another car.

This time I arrived in Colorado as a scholar rather than a tourist. I flew into Grand Junction bent upon documenting specific geologies and seeking out some original Midland artifacts that I had reason to believe still existed. I rented a car and drove around photographing buttes and mesas—scenery that looked exactly like the layout's. I drove south along the border between Colorado and Utah, imagining that I was a surveyor for the Midland who was looking for a route to Arizona. Then I doubled back and headed east along the Colorado River, following the tracks that the Midland had once shared with the Denver & Rio Grande.

In Rifle, I parked at a level crossing and tried to conjure up the ghost of an old Midland locomotive rumbling toward me, pouring smoke. No luck. For one thing, the scene wasn't in black and white. For another, reminders of modern life were everywhere: trucks blowing by on Interstate 70, a fast-food restaurant, the contrail of a jet. I had seen a couple of trains, but they were modern freights, a mile long and hauled by three or four diesels.

As I drove farther east to Basalt, and the sky turned from blue to gray, the past began to assert itself. It was in Basalt that the Midland's main line, coming downhill from Hagerman Pass, had once joined the Aspen spur; its yard was the one Rolf modeled for our layout. After poking around a bit, I found the eating house, which was essentially unchanged from the way it was pictured in the Cafky book. Even the distinctive trim band that connected the sills of the second-floor windows was still there. In the old Midland yard, the eating house had stood by itself, like an island among the tracks; now it was hemmed in by trees and parked cars. A sign out front indicated a boutique on the ground floor and a law firm above. A light rain began to fall, and two young couples hurried by me into the boutique. For a moment I imagined that they were going in to eat, and that the food was already there, on the long tables.

My last stop of the day was at the Colorado Railroad Museum in Golden. I arrived at closing time, but they let me in anyway. I wandered out behind the museum building into a meadow, where locomotives and cars sat on sidings. Some were derelict, others in various stages of restoration. Weeds and grasses grew knee-high between the rails. A passenger car caught my attention. I climbed aboard and closed the door behind me. Inside, the air was stale, as if it had been trapped in there for years. I eased into a seat, and its dry rattan crackled under my weight.

It was one of the Midland's cars. I sat for a while, wishing I had been around a hundred years earlier, in the railroad's heyday. I knew what the Durango to Silverton trip had been like— jolting and rocking along the rough rail, the smell of coal smoke and pine trees in the mountain air—and now I closed my eyes and began to turn the pages of the Cafky book in my mind, tracing the Midland's route from Colorado Springs as it left town, then swung west through Ute Pass into the heart of the Rockies. Here was that first steep ascent through Manitou and Cascade to Divide, with the valley floor dropping away below. The high mountain plateau at Hartsel appeared next, with the flatland stretching to the base of distant mountains. Then a succession of turns as the train descended, brake shoes squealing, along a boulder-strewn hillside, past the Buena Vista station (where a stagecoach waited to take passengers into town) and over a steel trestle. Something caught my eye, and I looked across the aisle to see John and Rolf, their backs to me as they peered out the window.

At Wild Horse the forty-mile climb northwest to the Continental Divide was launched from a plateau dotted with sagebrush, and soon I imagined the valleys of the Saguache Range unfolding ahead. Turns offered glimpses of the track: a thin line, a slight intervention in the land, disappearing here and there into short tunnels or dense stands of pine, but always climbing. The sky was a great dome of blue springing from purple mountains, the air was growing thinner, my eyes were dazzled by the sunlight. Past the Leadville spur, still climbing, crawling through a wooded valley. Then we rumbled across the great curving trestle, doubling back, now, with the valley dropping away on the other side. The High Line! All at once we were in the Hagerman Tunnel, and fumes were seeping in through the windows. The tunnel ended, and I was squinting again in the unfiltered sunlight. Eleven thousand five hundred feet—but that was the top, and now we were starting down, past the barren rock cleft at Hell Gate, then on through the tight switchbacks at Nast, where the tracks could been seen eight hundred feet below, winding down into a valley among tall trees, mostly dead, which stood like bare poles among house-sized boulders. At Ruedi a grassy valley appeared, and soon the train was coasting beside the sparkling green water of the Frying Pan River. We drifted on past the familiar cliffs by the quarry at Peach Blow and into Basalt, where the eating house came into view.

I stood up and the rattan crackled. John and Rolf had vanished. There was more to the Midland route, of course (in my mind it now extended all the way to Arizona), but that would have to wait for another time. I climbed down the steel steps and started to walk away. Then I turned and looked back at the car, now a shadowy form in the dusk. Vertical wood siding, dark green. The paint blistered. The trucks showing some rust. But its number—29—was legible, and the car looked ready to roll. Too bad the tracks that were once its home had been torn up, and the railroad that it served was gone.

IN THE ZONE

My trip to Colorado had been strange, with the things I imagined from the Midland's past superimposing themselves on the Colorado of today. The morning after I returned home, I went down the stairs to the basement, flipped on the light switches, and saw the world I had been imagining on my trip right in front of me. To be sure, this fictitious world was largely unfinished, but the trip west had given me a connection to the past that I was confident would guide me in the future.

I had stopped work on the layout in the spring, regretting that I couldn't finish a ravine that I had just begun. Another two weeks would have done it, but time had run out. Now it was fall, and I knew that my expanding career with ABC was going to be interrupting my work on the layout during the winter. Rolf couldn't start for a couple of weeks—he was negotiating to buy back the hobby shop—and as I stood looking at the neat stacks of plywood and blue foam, the clean brushes, and the well-swept basement floor, it made me weary to think of pulling everything out all over again and going to work by myself.

I had just bought an instruction book by a modeler named Malcolm Furlow, and in it were directions for building (from scratch, not from a kit) wooden trestles similar to the Midland's on the High Line. I knew Rolf would do a better job, but I decided to fill this hiatus by trying to build a trestle myself. Intricate as these structures were, Malcolm made assembling them seem simple. In fact, his book made everything look easy. Although he credited the influence of John Allen, his approach was far lighter.

For the book project, Malcolm had constructed a medium-sized layout, eight by ten feet, photographing each stage as he went along. He drew his inspiration from the narrow gauge railways of Colorado's San Juan Mountains mining region, which lay just to the east of our mythical Midland extension. We were modeling similar terrain, and Malcolm had a handy technique for just about everything. He didn't suffocate you with instructions, and he had a knack for getting the idea across with a couple of photos and a caption.

My trestle went together so quickly and looked so good I built another one. In the evenings, I made pine trees based on another of Malcolm's designs. Before long, Rolf was back—and so was my eagerness to tackle the ravine.

It sliced through from the front edge of the platform to the back wall, a distance of about seven feet. Part of Judy's Loop ran along its right side. Unfortunately, the bottom of the ravine was so narrow that it left me nowhere to stand comfortably while I built up the banks. As Malcolm Furlow would say, "Oops." I couldn't attack from the back because the tracks, and the basement's ten-inch-thick concrete outer wall, were in the way. My only choice was to balance in the streambed with one foot in front of the other, like one of the Egyptians painted on King Tut's tomb.

I'd climb onto the platform, and then, bending down to keep from hitting my head on the heating ducts above, saw away at the foam. It was a race to see if I could finish a section before the pain in my back forced me to take a break—the mountain range John Allen called the Akinbaks was being reborn. When Rolf suggested a quarry for the ravine's right side, I almost declined. But then I realized that I could make it simply by cutting into the foam, literally "quarrying" it with a kitchen knife, and the quarry was finished in a day. Ellen mixed a beautiful peach color for the newly exposed rock face, Rolf whipped up some structures, including a loading dock and a derrick, and the ravine days were over.

We decided to relocate the control panel, positioning it at the far left end of the layout, beyond the yard, so that the person operating the trains wouldn't interrupt the view of people watching them. The new control panel called for rewiring the entire layout, and Rolf spent two weeks under the plywood platform, working on his back in cramped quarters, without ever losing his sense of humor. When he finished, he filled a notebook with elegant diagrams of what he had done.

In the center of the panel was a schematic of the track plan. It showed the two concentric loops (John's and mine), the reverse loops, the yard, and all the sidings. Two power packs flanked the panel. Buttons controlled the switches (twenty-eight in all), while toggles determined the direction of the current in the eighteen power blocks. Our new control panel was handsome, but the real beauty was hidden beneath it, where Rolf's color-coded wires converged from all over the layout.

One afternoon, Rolf showed John how the system operated. John was in fifth grade and had moved to a new school. He was a conscientious student who felt the weight of his homework, and we hadn't seen much of him in the basement. I watched him nodding as Rolf went through the same explanation he had given me. Then they began to run the trains, starting with the basic maneuvers. Soon they had several trains running, and then they began to show off, changing loops and directions. One of the loops was a figure eight, which added to the complexity.

They assembled the trains in the yard using one of the little switchers, then coupled them to powerful road engines summoned from the roundhouse. The completed trains would ease out of the yard, pause at the station, and then set off for the far end of the basement. Moving at a scale speed of 25 mph, a train took more than two minutes to traverse one of the loops. Mountains hid its return trip, so the impression was of a train going from one place to another. Once it was back at the yard, the train could be switched to the other loop, and it would be another two minutes before it was back at the station. If one train was lapping clockwise, another could be going counterclockwise—but only with some tense moments as the two trains approached the same section of track from opposite directions. A third train could be circling Judy's Loop, which was still run from its separate power pack in its own private drawer.

In one session, John grasped the essence of how the layout worked. I never really got the hang of it. I had been brought up with the simplicity of operation made possible by Lionel's third rail, and while I understood the concept of reverse polarity that went with HO's two-rail setup, I got lost in the execution. All those toggles! But I didn't mind; a single train running through the landscape was thrilling enough for me.

As work progressed, John and I became curious about other local layouts. Curious—and apprehensive. With all that we were doing, I knew I would feel deflated if here, on our doorstep, someone was far ahead of us. Of course, I had already seen Don Buckley's terrific layout, but with its smaller scale and urban motif it defied direct comparison.

John told me that a friend of his was building a layout—or, rather, his father was building it for him. His dad was a wood-worker originally from Maine, a master craftsman of the sort whose work gets published in *Wooden Boat,* and he had the skill and temperament to do something really good. But when John visited his friend, he reported back that the layout was small, all on one level, and it had no scenery.

Dave Townsend's layouts (he had two, in different parts of his basement) were a bigger threat. Rolf had worked on them for years and referred to them frequently. Dave had built his older layout in a part of the basement that was badly lit and had too low a ceiling, but his new one occupied a large, brightly lit room, with the tracks zigzagging up the walls. I had been proud of my Furlow-inspired trestles, but they were nothing compared with the variety and quality of Dave's bridges. His layout wasn't better or worse than ours; like Don Buckley's, it was just *different.* I could relax.

After our spy trips, John and I no longer thought of our layout in a vacuum. We started to look hard at others that had been published in magazines, especially *Model Railroader.* When they covered a layout, they did it in style. The format included four or five large color photographs, a track diagram rendered by an artist, a short biography of the modeler, and an article. As each new issue came out, we studied the layouts with a mixture of excitement and anticipation, aware that as long as Rolf was on the job much of what we were seeing was within our reach to copy or adapt.

As our collection of *Model Railroaders* grew, I realized that virtually every issue featured a remarkable layout. Who were these guys? All along, I had thought the battle was with John Allen, but it was suddenly obvious I had been half asleep. A whole new generation of modelers had arisen, seemingly from nowhere, and they were building layouts that were in the same league as Allen's. A Boston man named George Sellios had modeled a city of breathtaking complexity. A Disney "imagineer," John Olson, was a master of the Western motif. The owner of a recording studio in Seattle, Paul Scoles, modeled the Northern California wilderness brilliantly and took his photographs from unusual angles. All of these men had ambition and the skills to go with it.

Of course, the new materials were a big part of the story. They made Rolf's job and mine easier—and everyone else's, too. John Allen had built his track by hand, cutting out each tie and spiking down the rails just as real railroad crews did. Now we had Flextrak. Allen had created his own trees and bushes, mostly from natural materials found by hunting around outside his house. Now a company called Woodland Scenics supplied everything, much of it synthetic, that you needed to "scenic" (that was the word) your layout. Rock molds? Woodland Scenics had them ready-made. Tunnel portals? All you had to do was choose between concrete, wood, or stone. The new instruction books such as Malcolm Furlow's were written by men who wanted things to be fast and easy. Taking forty-eight hours to model a cliff two feet long, as Linn Westcott had, was no longer something to be proud of.

Photography had become nearly as important as the modeling. *Model Railroader* ran a monthly feature called "Trackside Photos" in which some shots were computer-enhanced—a new direction for the hobby. Many of the newer layouts were being designed, it seemed, around a sequence of photo ops.

I was looking for something closer to the feeling you would get from seeing a large painting. I wanted you to reach the bottom of the basement stairs, and when you turned to look at the layout . . . Bam! You'd take in the whole thing, all sixty feet of it, in one glance.

Now it was fall, and the interruptions of the previous winter made me feel that we had somehow slipped behind a schedule I had promised myself didn't exist. I had big plans, and executing them called, once again, for a visit from Bill Berry. But this time Bill wasn't in the basement for just a couple of days, he worked for three weeks. He extended the backdrop the full length of the layout. He installed a valance and a false ceiling. This new ceiling hid the heating ducts, and painting it blue transformed it into a sky. Bill expanded the platform at the north end. And then he moved the post.

No big layout is complete without a post in the way somewhere. Even John Allen had one (which he tried to disguise as a chimneylike rock with a restaurant on top—one of his few bad ideas). Ours was near the ravine and about six inches behind the tracks that ran across the front of the layout. I had tried to mask the post behind a sheer rock cliff, but this hadn't worked out. I talked to my contractor friend Dick Coon and my brother David (who had drawn the framing plans for the house), and they agreed that we could move the post about ten inches without having the living room come crashing down through the sky. Ten inches! That such a small amount could seem like so much to me was evidence of how immersed I had become in the world of HO scale, where ten inches meant over seventy-two feet. That was *huge*.

Dick sent two extra men to help Bill. The plan was to install a new post, then remove the old one. They soon had the new post in, but the old one wouldn't budge. Bill elected to saw it in half. The post, however, was made of steel filled with concrete, and the sawing went slowly. If anyone questioned the value of having three first-class carpenters spend two hours moving a post less than a foot so that a foam cliff could look a little more realistic on an unfinished model train layout, he kept it to himself. When the pole was finally severed, Bill dragged the two halves out of the basement triumphantly, as if they were the bodies of enemy warriors slain in battle.

We also installed a new furnace. The old one had something amiss with its starting mechanism, which meant that Rolf and I would hear the roar of the igniter (basically a small flamethrower) and then, instead of the furnace coming to life, it would turn off, emit a few clicks, then try again. It was easy to imagine unburned oil vapor accumulating and the whole thing blowing up. The new unit was half the size and twice as efficient. Its on/off cycles, instead of being a test of nerves, were soothing. The thing purred like one of our locomotives.

I finished the cliff near the pole, then moved to the layout's other end. I would leave the center part for last; I liked the idea of the finished work growing from the ends toward the middle—it reminded me of the way the Transcontinental Railroad was built in the 1860s. Perhaps, like the men of the Central Pacific and the Union Pacific, Rolf and I would someday drive a golden spike and have a party.

The composition of the south end had evolved from the original four-by-eight-foot layout, and in building it I had wrestled with unfamiliar materials and techniques. The main idea had been trying to figure out how to make things look real, and I hadn't worried much about the artistic merits of what I was doing. Plenty of time for that, I had thought, looking along the large expanse of unfinished platform. Now the left-hand, south side was virtually finished, and I was about to commit to a plan for the north side.

I reviewed the photos of the great landscapes along the Midland route, but in the end I chose to copy the composition of the grim, brooding scene that was on the cover of John Allen's book. It superimposed itself onto the north end's barren plywood platform just as naturally as the Midland's yard at Basalt had fit the south end. My trestles led into the scene from the left; they looked as if they had been built, from the beginning, just to fit the new scheme.

The south end of the layout was about eight feet deep, while the north end was fully twelve feet from the front edge to the back wall. Having learned a lesson in the ravine, I wanted easy access to everything. I designed a high mountain ridge that acted as a screen for a small open space behind it, where I could stand to build yet another layer of scenery—scenery I didn't want to tackle until the more important front elements were in place. To get to this space, I left a slot in the mountain. To navigate this slot, I had to step up eighteen inches onto the platform, then turn and shuffle sideways through the mountain while at the same time bending down to get under the top of the ridge. Ordinarily, this would have been easy, but then an unforeseen complication arose.

During the previous spring, I had begun to suffer from dizzy spells. They usually struck while I was out jogging, but they had also occurred while I was working on the ravine. Now they were attacking more frequently, and often they were triggered by the awkward maneuvers required to traverse the slot. At least once a day, I found myself sitting on the basement floor waiting for the dizziness to clear up, worried about what might be wrong and frustrated by the interruption of work. It was unnerving, and I went to Dr. Gott to see if he could tell me what was wrong. He said he wanted to start with a heart test, so I spent twenty-four hours with a device called a Holter monitor strapped to my chest. The Holter's divinations concluded that my heart was not to blame, which cheered me up and for the time being lessened my concerns about the dizziness.

The design for Mount Whitman (named after my friend John) called for a mass of plywood, foam, chicken wire, and plaster fourteen feet across at the base and rising five feet from the platform to an overall height of almost seven feet. Unlike the smaller mountains, which were solid foam, Mount Whitman's core was to be comprised of plywood steps, like a ziggurat. In less than a week I ran through a whole stack of four-by-eight-foot plywood. Converting that wood into a mountain was some of the sloppiest work I had done so far.

I jammed the Skilsaw in the wood so often that a pall of blue smoke hung in the air, and I repeatedly snapped the blades of the band saw. Because I never did anything right the first time, or the second, each new piece of the mountain required multiple fittings. I made the trip from the band saw to the mountain and back hundreds of times, threading my way past tables and sawhorses, and over blue foam, orange extension cords, and jagged pieces of leftover wood. I became so familiar with the route I no longer looked where I was stepping.

To fasten the plywood together, I made pilot holes with a portable electric drill and then used an electric screwdriver to install Sheetrock screws. They augured into the wood as fast as I could have driven a nail. The drill's sound was a nasty *eeeooOOOWWWWW,* and the screwdriver answered with *EEEeeeuuunnck,* the two tools having a plaintive conversation. With no fear that craftsmanship might rear its ugly head, I could do the sawing, drilling, and screwing almost without conscious thought, directly translating my ideas into physical fact. People who stopped by found it difficult to distinguish between the mountain and the mess that surrounded it. But I didn't care.

Sawingdrillingscrewing, or was it screwingdrillingsawing? I paid no attention. Not surprisingly, this led to mistakes, but when something needed to be corrected, I had only to resort to a ferocious tool called the Sawz-All. Gripping it firmly, and holding it low at my hip, like a lance, I would advance toward the offending area. The saw's design made it easy to do what seemed impossible, which was to begin cutting wood in the *center* of a piece, rather than along one of its edges. I just aimed the short, strong, pointed blade at the wood, then kept a firm grip as, splinters flying, it battered open a ragged hole. The vibration was so great it shook Rolf's buildings at Cielo Vista, almost a (scale) mile away.

Once the mountain was complete I began designing a mine. Most of the Colorado mines were immense structures, and replicating them in HO scale would have taken up most of the north end. I needed the sense of a big mine without its size. Evening after evening, I made sketches that had all the ingredients: the square tower, the tall, black smokestack, the conical mound of tailings, the cribbing. Finally I got something I liked, so I built a cardboard model and placed it on the layout. For once, a building looked too small.

The mine was at the base of a tall rock cliff, which dwarfed it, and if I enlarged the mine enough to compete with the cliff it would be out of scale with everything else. But scale is relative . . . what if the mine had something *it* could tower over? Rolf and I pulled out the stores that John had made and lined them up along with a bank and a saloon that Gerry Bill had given me, creating a town that we positioned down the slope, below the mine. The change was immediate: the mine now loomed above the little town. We laid out a road on the steep hill between them, full of switchbacks, and the mine appeared even higher up and more distant. Success.

At the same time, I was learning about other tricky optical situations. For example: clouds painted on a layout backdrop look all wrong in a photograph unless the camera is positioned at exactly ninety degrees to the backdrop. If you photograph them at an angle, the clouds appear in perspective—which they never do in real life. The solution? A sky that was flat blue (it's like that much of the time in Colorado, anyway). The next challenge was water. Bill McClanahan's book had listed eight ways to simulate water, and only one, his least favorite, was to use water itself. That's because real water doesn't move at scale speed. Also, model streams are rarely deeper than a saucer, and water that shallow is virtually transparent, although dyeing it can help.

I worked on Christmas Day, unwilling to sever my connection with the layout. All December, I had been lucky; areas kept inventing themselves, as if they had been waiting for me in some parallel universe. I was being drawn into a fantasy world that was becoming increasingly real every day. I remembered a letter John Allen had written a few weeks before his death: "Been pushing up the line from Great Divide to Angel's Camp . . ." He had crossed into a twilight zone in which what he modeled no longer referred to an external reality—it referred only to itself. Now I, too, was in the zone.

By mid-January, the north end was nearly finished. The slot had vanished beneath layers of chicken wire and shop rags soaked in plaster. I was working more and more quickly. I had discovered joint compound, a plasterlike material ordinarily used to fill cracks and dents in walls. It came in small tubs and could be troweled into place like icing, functioning as both a filler and a glue. A gap between pieces of foam? Reach for the joint compound. Want to hold a rock in place on a slope? Ditto. Twigs, sawdust, and leftover bits of wood and foam could be combined with joint compound wherever I wanted rough terrain. Spraying it with water produced authentic gullies and erosion—eons of aging in an instant. Picasso once said that what made him good at painting was that he "did it worse every day." If that was true, I was headed in the right direction.

As my memory of Dave Townsend's bridges faded, my trestles began to look better. The bigger one, about eighteen inches high, was curved, banked, and went downhill. The smaller, about thirteen inches high, was also curved. The abutments were simulated stone, made from urethane castings. The scenery around them was made with my new joint compound technique and looked as if it had been thrown together in haste by a giant. Which, in a sense, it had been.

At the end of January, I unplugged the phone. It wasn't only that calls were taking up too much time, I just didn't want to know about the outside world. I rarely left the house. Day after day I wore the same blue New York Giants sweatpants, the same sweater. Our local hardware store was delivering sheets of plywood and foam on a regular schedule. UPS and FedEx trucks frequented our driveway. Rolf arrived each morning to find me at work and left in the evening with me still working. I regarded him as a migrating bird, with our basement just one stop in the routine of his day. The only time I looked outside was when I surfaced for lunch, and then the weather, whatever it was, barely registered. I was in Colorado, in the summer, where the sky was always blue.

Occasionally, a momentary flash of self-awareness made me wonder what I had gotten into. After all, somewhere out there people were pursuing useful careers and doing good deeds. In the time it took me to build half a mountain, some Wall Streeter was making enough money to buy a BMW. I didn't care. Day after day, I just aimed straight ahead, like a man hacking his way through a jungle, improvising with each stroke. I never thought that some wisdom, or cosmic insight, might be lurking in the matrix of decisions and events that had led me to this basement obsession, but I was convinced that if I stopped, something bad would happen.

I was having trouble seeing things close up and bought a pair of reading glasses. Now I was more conscious of detail than I had been. The combination of seeing better and having some areas nearly finished made me wonder: How good is good enough? In my Lionel days, anything I might have done would have been fatally compromised by the third rail and the sharp turns, but now no limits to realism existed beyond those of my own ingenuity. How about more trees, more bushes, more ground cover, some extra details?

All the landscape materials I needed, along with the tools to install them, were ranged on a table pulled up next to the layout. Like a surgeon or a chef, I had everything at hand, and if I couldn't find something, Rolf could. I had textures such as sand and gravel—twelve grades of gravel, and now, with my glasses, I could tell the differences among them. To apply color, I had chalks, cans of spray paint, and acrylics. I had brushes, sponges, spray bottles, tape, files, rags, and several different glues, including men's hair spray, which I misted over finished areas to hold everything in place. To anyone else, the table was chaotic; to me it was a secretly coded staging area full of treasures.

Nature reproduces itself in different scales, and I was starting to think HO must be one of them. Twigs of real trees were ready-made HO trunks, pebbles from the driveway became boulders, saw cuts were crevices. About the smallest things I could expect my fingers to work with were the parts and pieces of HO buildings. Figures looked real with remarkably few details. Working day after day in HO made me think that a successful world could be created at this scale . . . and made me wonder, too, if our idea of 1:1 being "real" wasn't perhaps a bit presumptuous—surely a world could exist that was eighty-seven times *bigger* than ours.

The next step was to see how the scenes looked with Colorado Midland trains. Unhappily, they were not available from ordinary retail sources. Midland locomotives had never been modeled by a major manufacturer such as Bachmann or Rivarossi. You couldn't buy one in Rolf's shop, or even at the Red Caboose in New York. But they did exist.

The source was a group of collectors who bought and sold custom locomotives that rarely appeared in catalogs, even Walthers's. These engines were made from brass, a soft metal that lends itself to the manufacture of detailed castings (plus brass can be soldered, which is a simpler process than welding). Rolf remembered having seen a brass Midland locomotive somewhere, and now he began writing and calling around.

In the steam era, the manufacturers of real locomotives built basic models that they adapted to the specific requirements of their customers. Each railroad operated differently and over different routes; most were willing to spend extra money for features that their technical people believed would improve performance. In 1915, the Baldwin Locomotive Works, the largest in the country, offered more than five thousand designs.

By contrast, mass-produced model locomotives were customized merely by changing decals. The slight mechanical differences that told such a fascinating story in real life were ignored so that the cost of developing the model could be amortized over several thousand units. To further limit costs, mass-produced model locomotives were made from a combination of relatively cheap materials, typically cast metal and styrene. Brass locomotives, on the other hand, were built in runs of twenty-five to fifty, just like the real thing, and they were wonderfully heavy and furiously detailed. In the world of brass, cost wasn't a factor. Rolf had seen locomotives sell for $4,000.

After several months, his search for Midland locomotives hit the jackpot. First, a man walked into his store with one for sale, and just days later, Rolf went to a model train show and found another. Fortunately, thanks to the relative simplicity of the original Midland design, these cost in the hundreds of dollars, not the thousands.

Each was what is referred to as a 2-8-0, which meant it had two small pilot wheels at the front, eight driving wheels (four per side), and no wheels at the back under the cab. But they looked quite different. With the Cafky book in hand, Rolf was able to identify one as part of a series of five (numbers 201–205) that Baldwin had built for the Midland in 1901. Rolf chose to number ours 202. In real life, 202 had tall driving wheels (sixty inches) and an unusual double-cylinder arrangement that, within a few months of delivery, began to leak so much steam that the engineers had trouble seeing the track ahead. The other locomotive, also by Baldwin, was one of a series of six built for the Midland in 1907. Not surprisingly, the railroad by then had instructed Baldwin to revert to a single-cylinder setup. The driving wheels were smaller (fifty-two inches), even though the locomotive, overall, was somewhat bigger and heavier (193,000 pounds versus 182,000 pounds).

Rolf painted the locomotives and delivered them to the layout. They were so perfect I was reluctant to touch them. John came down for a look and felt the same way. Tentatively, we tested one, then the other. Neither ran as well as one of our ordinary diesels. I began to worry that the pursuit of historical accuracy might be costing us the fun we once had running the trains. But John was twelve, and had less and less time for trains anyway.

With the locomotives finished, Rolf began purchasing kits for the rolling stock: passenger cars, boxcars, cattle cars, flatcars, cabooses. He found decals with the Midland logo. He did the assembly in a back room at Berkshire Hills, and every few weeks he would show up with a box full of newly completed cars.

The arrival of each fresh batch triggered a frenzy of photography. The trains looked good at the roundhouse, in the yard, in front of the station, backing down the siding to Newman's Own, in the shadow of the canyon, and crossing the trestles—especially crossing the trestles, where the spirit of the old High Line was evoked anew. I no longer feared that *my* fun with the layout was over.

By now, I had taken hundreds of pictures. A few managed to convey a sense of the landscape, but none did justice to the new Midland engines and cars. Even with help from my friends at the camera store, I just couldn't capture the intricate detailing of the new equipment. I was used to hiring professionals who special-

ized in architectural photography to record my buildings; now it
was time to find someone to shoot the trains.

Dave Frary was my man. I had seen his pictures in *Model
Railroader* and knew that he photographed other layouts in addition to his own. He was a lobster fisherman who lived in Swampscott, Massachusetts, just a three-hour drive from Sharon. The
pictures of his layout, the Carrabasset and Dead River, were suf-
fused with light that was so real you thought he must have photographed the layout outside.

Dave was in the phone book. He listened as I outlined the situation—and said he couldn't do it. He explained that he was
under contract to *Model Railroader* and could shoot only for
them. I asked if there was anyone else he could recommend.
There wasn't. I was about to hang up when Dave suggested I call
Model Railroader to see if they would make an exception. He
gave me the name of a friend of his who worked for the magazine, Jim Kelly.

I checked the masthead, and it didn't take long to see that Jim
Kelly was the managing editor. I called, said Dave had given me
his name, and told him about my layout.

"The Colorado Midland," Jim repeated thoughtfully, "that's
unusual." He asked if we had any pictures. I said we did, but explained that I wasn't much of a photographer and that the layout
wasn't finished. He suggested that I mail him the pictures anyway. If he liked them, he'd consider sending Dave.

"Who knows," Jim Kelly said, "we might be interested in an
article on your layout."

ithin a week, Jim Kelly phoned back. He liked our pictures, and it was agreed that Dave Frary would photograph the layout—in just four weeks. This was short notice, but I wasn't about to ask for a postponement.

Rolf and I made a list. We knew that many of the typical *Model Railroader* shots were loaded with detail and told a story, so we began ordering sheds, outhouses, wagons, carriages, signs, and telegraph poles. We bought dozens of miniature animals, including a herd of galloping buffalo that I positioned at the edge of a cliff, pursued by an Apache on horseback. Rolf installed ducks wading at the edge of a stream. Out behind Newman's Own, we created a small graveyard for the unlucky employees who had been forced to taste-test the company's products. (A fresh grave had a coffin next to it, awaiting interment.) We scratched paths along the ground to suggest that people took shortcuts between the buildings. We put signs on walls, had men delivering a piano to the saloon, broke some of the pickets in a fence, and scattered junk out behind the engine house.

Rolf cast his gimlet eye everywhere. He knew that a certain kind of detail, relating to the correctness of the railroad itself, must not be overlooked, and for a while mild-mannered Rolf became so focused I realized the best thing for me to do was stay out of his way. He spent several days painting the sides of the rails to make them look rusty, and he also rusted up the sidings, where the trains rarely run. He stacked replacement rails at appropriate intervals along the line. He ordered switch stands. The Midland had water-filled barrels on their wooden trestles, used for putting out fires started by sparks from the locomotives, so he bought barrels a quarter inch high, painted them red, and glued them to tiny cantilevered platforms. He invited Dave Townsend to come over and critique the layout. Dave brought his airbrush and sprayed a thin haze of black above each tunnel opening to suggest smoke and soot. Rolf didn't ask for my approval for any of this—he just did it. He knew Dave Frary was a pro, and Rolf wasn't going to let us look bad. When he was finished, I could see that the layout looked subtly different—more authentic.

Dave Frary told me he would come in late afternoon, take a look around, then start shooting the next morning. By the appointed time, Rolf and I had put all the tools away, unclipped the work lights, coiled the extension cords, and swept the floor. Dave was late, but it was snowing so we assumed it was slow going out there on the roads. This was a moment to stand back and enjoy the progress we had made in the last month, but we gave the layout only a quick glance; if something was wrong it was too late to fix it.

The doorbell rang. Dave was a balding, bearded man with a round, friendly face and the rugged build you would expect of someone who hauled up eight hundred lobster traps every day. His equipment was neatly packed in three large cases, which we carried downstairs. He began to walk slowly along the layout, nodding but saying nothing. No reaction as he passed Frary's Carriages, a building we had named in his honor. He had photographed dozens of other layouts and was surely a veteran of moments like this, when people were apprehensively awaiting some sign of his approval. But if he sensed the drama, he gave no indication of it, and I had the impression that he was not appraising and judging as much as simply sizing up his photographic opportunities.

"It's nice," he said at last. "I see plenty to shoot." And then he asked where he could plug in his lights.

Dave came back early the next morning. I was ready to enjoy a full day of watching an expert at work, and I hoped to learn something, too. He had written a book, *How to Build Realistic Model Railroad Scenery,* and in the introduction he described his approach to modeling as methodical and formulaic, intended to produce predictable results time after time. As he unpacked the cases, it was obvious that his thoroughness extended to his photography.

He had a formidable array of camera bodies (both 35 mm and large-format four-by-five), tripods, lenses, lens shades, adapter rings, filters, gels, cable releases, meters, film holders, lights and light stands, flashes, fuses, and diffusers. And film, box after box of it. By the time all this was unpacked, I no longer thought I'd be asking Dave for photo tips: he was way over my head.

Like Rolf, Dave worked quickly but without haste. There

were angles I hoped he'd shoot, but I steeled myself to keep quiet. Dave was in our basement at *Model Railroader*'s expense, not mine, and my interests were best served by his taking the kind of shot he knew by long experience the magazine preferred—a wide-angle view intended to produce broad documentation of the layout. He also wanted the shots to be busy and to suggest action. (Model railroad photographs are taken with the locomotives stopped, but the idea is to fool the eye into thinking they are moving.)

In his first shot, near Newman's Own, he used three trains. In his second, at the station, he filled the platform with figures. Once Dave decided on a shot and was setting up the lighting, Rolf positioned the trains, and I could see that he took quiet pride in running them to the location under their own power. Then he checked the wheels. (From our own shots, we knew that in even a cursory glance at a picture you will spot a wheel off the tracks.) Finally he added figures, sticking them to the ground with tiny balls of mortician's wax. Dave took test shots with Polaroid film, and I scrutinized these with a magnifying glass to make sure nothing was missing or looked out of place.

In midafternoon, Dave moved to the north end, shooting the trestles. So far, his lighting effects had simulated broad daylight, with plenty of fill to minimize the shadows, but as he studied the mine and the canyon behind it, he recognized the influence of John Allen and decided to try a shot that, like one of Allen's, would create a specific mood. His idea was for the mountain slopes in the foreground to be in shadow, with sunlight seeping through the canyon from the valley beyond. A few rays would strike the silvery metal roof of the mine, which was to be the focal point. He began crawling back and forth under the layout, dragging lights and special gels to the open area behind the mountain.

When he had the lighting the way he wanted it, the effect of a pale dawn was so convincing that it was difficult to remember that just four months before, this had been nothing but plywood and chicken wire.

In late April, I was back in Colorado, in a suburb of Denver, writing a television script for an independent production company. I wrote in pencil on a yellow legal pad, and after a couple of days I noticed that I'd get about halfway across a line, then have to change the angle of the pad because my hand wouldn't continue smoothly across the page. Thinking it was a cramp, I rubbed my hand, then went outside and walked around the building. It was a fine spring day. The parking lot was edged with yellow flowers, and the sky was as blue as the layout's. The clear air made the snowcapped Rockies appear closer than they really were, as if I were seeing them through a telephoto lens. I knew that hidden in the mountains were towns like Leadville and Aspen that the Midland had once connected to the outside world.

When I went back inside, the cramping hadn't gone away. My fingers seemed to be misaligned, as if some internal twisting force had torqued them out of their normal relationship with my arm and even my body. I had a fleeting sense that my brain was trying to straighten things out and not quite connecting with my hand; the unsuccessful effort made my chest tighten up, as if I were out of breath. I tried to persuade myself it was just the altitude.

A week later, I was in Indianapolis to cover the Indy 500. ABC placed great importance on their telecast of this event. (Even though I was doing more than twenty shows a year, many of which had nothing to do with automobile racing, it was my performance at Indy that counted whenever my contract was up for renewal.) I always stayed at the Speedway Motel, which was on the grounds of the track, in the shadow of the grandstand at Turn Two.

Each year, opening the door to my room at the motel meant I would be closing off the rest of my life for a month, until the 500 was over. In that month, I immersed myself in the statistics, lore, and nuance of an event I had raced in once myself, and loved. But now I was anxious; the cramping that had begun in Colorado was worse, and my right shoulder was slumping. I was unaccountably tired. As the days went by, I spent less time in the pits and garages and more time hanging out in the sanctuary of the TV compound. And I often left the compound even before practice was over, to go back to my room to rest. In previous years, the spare bed would be blanketed with pages of notes; now I had only a few.

The overarching requirement for work in sports television is not what you say or even how you look; it is your energy—and mine was clearly down. I couldn't discuss this with anyone in Indianapolis because if word filtered back to ABC, they would in all likelihood find someone to replace me. A few days before the race, I made a short trip home and went to see Dr. Gott. Peter had not stopped puzzling over my dizzy spells, and he was ready with a new idea: a brain scan. A *brain* scan? Just to rule out the possibility of a tumor, he said. A *tumor*? Having the scan would mean delaying my return to Indy for a day, and I was so wrapped up with my preparations for the race I almost said no. But I knew the possibility of a brain tumor was not something to be ignored, even for the Indy 500.

At the local hospital, they stuck me in the MRI tube, and when it was over the technician, a racing fan, gave me the thumbs-up; whatever was wrong wasn't showing up on his screen. I went back for the 500, still having difficulty writing, but feeling such a wave of relief and optimism that I didn't care. Whatever this was all about could wait.

After the race, however, I again felt bad, only now I couldn't hope my troubles might somehow be blamed on the tension surrounding Indy. To relax, I found myself going down to the basement to watch the trains. Around and around they ran, the engines hauling the rows of cars, everything working exactly as it was designed to.

Another trip to Peter Gott. This time, he sent me to a young neurologist, who examined me and then told me that while many things were possible, my symptoms were similar to those that were present in Parkinson's disease. He said this as calmly as if he were telling me I had crumbs on my sleeve. He assured me I was in no immediate danger, and that he wasn't 100 percent sure of his diagnosis. He suggested I see a specialist, and within a few days, I found myself in New York, in the office of Dr. Stanley Fahn. Dr. Fahn knew as much about Parkinson's as anyone, and after confirming that I did, indeed, have the disease, he agreed to take me on as a patient.

Parkinson's can take many forms, but they all mean one thing: loss of control over your body. You might have uncontrollable shaking of the hands and legs. You might stiffen up, and have a shuffling walk and stooped posture. In advanced stages, patients become utterly helpless. Drugs are available that can mask the symptoms early on, but as the disease worsens and more medication is required, patients may reach a point where the side effects outweigh the benefits. Naturally, I pressed Dr. Fahn for a timetable, but he refused to make predictions. He said the disease affects people in different ways, and that even tracking its course over several years was an unreliable indicator: the graph could spike at any time.

Gloomy as all this was, Ellen and I both sensed from what we were hearing that the doomsday stuff was at least three years away, maybe even five or more. A lucky few even lived out their lives with Parkinson's being nothing more than an inconvenience. The diagnosis and meeting Dr. Fahn had gone smoothly and quickly, but fully absorbing the reality of what I might someday face took me weeks and the help of a psychiatrist, Dr. Sandy Mirabile. Then one day I realized nothing remained that was fresh for me to confront, at least for now. The fear was still there, but it was always the same fear, so it had lost its edge.

Just in time, too. The bare trees and cold air outside meant the layout was waiting, in the cozy basement.

But I hesitated to resume work. I was learning to ignore Parkinson's, but I also didn't want to be foolish about my future. Maybe it was time to give up the layout. It had been photographed and would soon be published, so maybe this was a good time to call it quits. Painting. Architecture. I certainly had much that I wanted to do in those fields. Get on with that, while there was time.

My next thought was to finish the layout in a hurry. In the four years since Rolf had come on board, we had spent three seasons building the first third, but we had taken only one to complete the north end. At this accelerated rate, and assuming the upcoming winter went as well as the last one, our golden spike could be driven sometime next spring. But as I imagined the layout finished, I felt a void, a sense of loss. Building the railroad—the joys of planning the scenes with John, the excitement of having Rolf assure me that something I had assumed was beyond our reach was in fact "no problem," the delight of being able to ignore the outside world for weeks at a stretch—had been a wonderful part of my life, and I didn't want it to end, at least not yet.

Slow down, I decided. That last area of bare plywood was a nonrenewable resource.

olf was calling from his shop in Canaan—and trying unsuccessfully to control his excitement. The February issue of *Model Railroader* had just arrived. "The cover is a shot of your layout," he said. *Your* layout; Rolf, always modest.

"I'm on my way," I said.

He had the magazine on the counter. The cover showed our locomotive No. 202 crossing a trestle, with a steep cliff to the left and a square of sky and the mine to the right. No. 202 was steaming through our version of Colorado and out across America's newsstands. Inside were four more shots, including Dave's magically lit view of the mine.

The Gorre and Daphetid had shown me that a layout can be a stage set, but until I saw Dave's pictures in the magazine, I didn't appreciate the power a photograph can have to isolate a small part of the layout and transform it. The photograph stops at the edges of the shot. It allows you to focus all your energy on one particular spot, which just for the time you are making the picture can be specially lit and given a level of detail much higher than the surrounding area. Figures can be brought in to help tell the story. Suddenly I saw our layout as you would any real landscape—photogenic just as it is, or as a locale (or backdrop) for a specific event.

After seeing Dave's photos, I made up my mind to design the rest of the layout by composing the scenes through a viewfinder. His shots had shown me that our layout could be a tool for a kind of expression that I was eager to pursue. During the fall and early winter, I had been tied up with architecture. But in mid-January, just after the article came out, I was ready to go—and Rolf agreed to take some time away from the shop.

I had bought a box of paper masks, of the kind worn by doctors or people who work in the paint-spraying booths at body shops. It was pure superstition, but I couldn't shake the idea that working with the blue foam was somehow connected to my getting Parkinson's. Dr. Fahn didn't think so, but no one knew what caused the disease (was it hereditary? environmental?), and working with the foam was the only unusual thing that I could think of having done. I offered a mask to Rolf, who politely declined.

Proof of how addled my logic was: I had no intention of giving up the blue foam. It gave me a way to make our mountains, and I wasn't about to attempt something new.

I mounted our camera on a tripod and pointed it at the spot where I planned to build Englemann Canyon—out of blue foam.

Englemann Canyon was a dry gulch just up the slope from the town of Manitou, eleven miles northwest of Colorado Springs. Midland engineers had crossed the gulch with a curving iron viaduct 280 feet long and 50 feet high. Painted maroon, it was an ideal structure to be the focal point of the next section. But first, as with the mine, it was necessary to adapt the viaduct to the layout. We decided to have it span a river instead of a gulch, and to make it taller and not as long as the original. Our viaduct's vertiginous proportions would create an illusion of danger that would be echoed by reality: if a locomotive jumped the rails, the one-hundred-scale-foot plunge would wreck the engine and damage the bridge. It might even dent the Dolores, which was the name I was giving to the Masonite "river" that would flow under our viaduct. (I had seen the authentic Dolores on my visit to western Colorado.)

I was becoming increasingly fascinated by the subtle shifts between what was real and what wasn't. For example, our locomotives were true to the prototype in appearance and capable of pulling cars along tracks and climbing grades, but they did not run like real steam engines at all. Inside their bodies were electric motors, not boilers—and sometimes the motor wasn't even in the engine itself, it was in the tender. Rolf built a bridge that consisted of the same timbers (scaled down, of course) as its prototype, but owing to such mysterious (at least to me) laws of physics as the modulus of elasticity and the moment of inertia, our small bridge was far stronger, relatively, than its larger counterpart.

I wanted the locomotives and structures to be as authentic as possible so that, by proxy, they would connect the viewer with an actual world, even if it was a world that hadn't existed for one hundred years. In modeling the landscape, however, I thought hyperrealism was the wrong approach. Children too young to make the connection to the real thing can like a crude toy for its own sake—and often prefer it to one that, seen by adult eyes, is the more faithful replica. Bertrand Russell once observed that the essence of the ideal is not to be real, and I was intrigued by anomalies such as the way our fake trees produced real shadows and that to get real-looking water you used an epoxy resin called Envirotex. At our quarry, a dozen miniature workers struggled to lift a block of marble that was actually a tiny piece of Styrofoam so light it had to be glued down to keep from being blown away.

The layout stretched through the basement for roughly one scale mile. Nowhere in the real Colorado was there a mile of terrain that packed in the variety and excitement of what I was building; it had to be edited and compressed. I was inventing a basement cordillera and even a climate to go with it. I wanted my cliffs and meadows and rivers to be judged purely on what was emotionally correct, and to hell with the geology.

Spring came, and we wrapped up Englemann Canyon. I went back to another season as an ABC commentator, my twenty-first. The Parkinson's hadn't bothered me much during the winter in the basement—in fact, the sawing and drilling had been therapeutic, limbering up my hand. The dizzy spells had stopped; they had only been a warning that something was wrong. I was looking forward to Indy and the other races, confident that I would have an easier time than the year before. But I was in trouble from the start.

The tension of television exacerbated the Parkinson's symptoms, especially the most recent one, which was the shaking of my hands. Holding the microphone steady went from difficult to nearly impossible. At Indy, it was clear to everyone at ABC that I was going downhill, and at the end of the season the network declined to renew my contract. I found myself out of a job—but not for long. A new network called Speedvision, devoted entirely to racing, was happy to take me on.

Still, when November arrived, it felt good to leave the turbulence of the real world behind and reenter my invented one. The basement's embracing concrete walls represented stability that had been lacking in my life upstairs. I was back in control.

I threw away the masks, along with any idea that my fears of Parkinson's could force me to rush the layout to completion. I knew exactly what I wanted to do: finish the project in such a way as to have no regrets whatsoever. Rolf said he felt the same way. He had found someone to look after the store while he worked with me, and he was keen to see the layout to its successful conclusion no matter how long it took.

With this new perspective, I immediately saw that our town, Cielo Vista, wasn't big enough, or gritty enough, to truly evoke the sort of Old West frontier town—like Leadville—that John and I had envisioned back when we were just starting. We needed more buildings. A saloon. A bordello. A creaky wooden sidewalk. The call went out to Bill Berry, and he added eighteen inches to the layout in front of Cielo Vista. He had barely finished screwing in the last piece of plywood before I was there with the blue foam, making ground onto which we promptly extended Main Street. Instead of building new structures, we decided to transplant the little town at the base of the mine, which I had mistakenly positioned too far from the tracks to appear in any photograph that also included a train. (Rolf replaced it with a row of workers' cabins.) Adding to a highly detailed part of the layout that for years had been accepted as finished, and ripping out a whole town, loosened us up. Suddenly nothing seemed out of bounds.

As Rolf set to work on the town, I began to design the landscape that would sit squarely in the center of the final third of the layout—the last big scene left to build. I had used the best of John Allen, and now I turned to the photographs of the man who had inspired Allen: William Henry Jackson.

Jackson, who lived to be ninety-nine years old, had a face that seemed to have been cut from the same granite that appeared so often in his photographs. His forehead overhung his eyes like a protective cliff, his nose was large and straight, his skin was drawn tight against his cheekbones. Slightly built, he possessed a wiry strength that enabled him to haul his bulky cameras, glass plates, and chemicals up mountains and cliffs to vantage points from which he had the high, almost bird's-eye view you have when you stand looking at a model train layout.

He had been a staff artist for the Union Army during the Civil War, drawing vignettes of life in camp. Like many soldiers, he headed west when the war was over, arriving in California in 1866. After a brief stint in the goldfields, Jackson joined some cowboys who were heading back east with a herd of wild horses. He wound up in Omaha, where he and his brothers established a photographic studio. In 1869, he received a commission from the Union Pacific to photograph its newly completed transcontinental line. Two years later Jackson was in western Wyoming as the photographer for a geological survey that led to the creation of Yellowstone National Park. The 1880s saw him based in Denver and working for the Midland and other Colorado railroads, including the Denver & Rio Grande. His job was to help promote the new routes by taking pictures that documented the beauty and drama of the landscape through which they ran—

meaning that Jackson was always pointing his camera at exactly the sort of scene I wanted for the layout.

His travel arrangements were classy: a private train consisting of a locomotive and a special car fitted out with living quarters and a studio. Up and down the lines he went, setting his own schedule as he looked for the special effects that light and weather would provide. Jackson's Colorado was a virgin wilderness that was among the most beautiful and sublime landscapes anywhere, and he saw as much of it as any man.

He had an eye for texture and composition, skillfully contrasting mirror-smooth lakes with craggy rocks and framing snow-clad peaks with stunted foreground foliage. He photographed a snowstorm on Pike's Peak and shot from the bottom of the Black Canyon of the Gunnison. He photographed above the tree line and in caves. And he didn't confine himself to nature. He photographed the great mines of Colorado, including the Spring Gulch Mine and the Lixivator Smelter. He photographed the raw and rutted streets of Upper Creede and Cripple Creek. He was in Hagerman Pass during the winter of 1899, when the Midland was shut down for two and a half months, and he documented the railroad's struggle with the elements.

To capture the essence of Jackson's art in a single scene would be impossible—he left a life's work of more than eighty thousand photographs. But I found myself looking again and again at a shot that showed angular slabs of rock jutting like a wall into a river. Contrasting with the rocks' planar form was the strong linearity of lodgepole pines that seemed to be growing right out of the rocks. I would add cliffs on the far side and have a bridge across the top; the train crossing it would be silhouetted dramatically against the sky. A big vista; a perfect subject for William Henry Jackson. A scene that was inspired by a photograph was being designed to produce another photograph.

I got to work, but the layout's unfinished area was deceptively large, and I spent all that winter on just the part back near the wall, not even beginning to build the Jackson scene. The next winter was again cut short by other commitments, but I painted the river and carved the banks.

Subtly, the atmosphere in the basement changed. The clamor of ripping plywood was gone; we worked quietly, and the only sound was the new furnace discreetly turning itself on and off. A day's work that once meant roving from one end of the layout to the other, dragging along extension cords to power the saws and drills, now involved hovering over an area no bigger than a square foot—and sometimes less than that. Earlier, building mountains in a few days, I had been godlike. Now I was working at the scale and pace of an HO man.

When spring came, the scenery was complete all along the back, and visitors barely noticed the sole remaining unfinished section, about four by eight feet, at the front. When I began, four by eight feet was all there was—and it had seemed like so much! Now four by eight feet was again all there was—and it seemed like so little.

One season to go.

In the previous couple of years, one of my architectural projects had been the design of a new school for young kids (kindergarten through fourth grade). From the beginning, I felt a train layout was required. Not sure that the board of trustees would agree with me, I cagily labeled the place I planned to put it "storage" on the blueprints and kept quiet about my intentions.

Late one Friday afternoon in August, when construction was nearly finished and the crews were leaving for the weekend, I swooped in with my plywood and blue foam. By Monday, the layout was finished. Lilliputian, it was nonetheless full of action. The train emerged from a rock cliff, passed through a small town, then teetered across a stupendously high trestle before disappearing into a tunnel. A maxi-effect in a mini-space. It was set up so that when the kids pushed a button, the train did three laps before being shut down by an automatic timer. Rolf painted the school's initials on the locomotive, and the three-car train included a flatcar for messages, such as birthday greetings.

On the big layout, each different phase had taken months or even years to finish. But on the school's, I finished the plywood and track laying by the end of the first day, the mountains the next, and everything else on the third. Strange: in more than fifty years of infatuation with model trains, I had never completed a layout, and yet now I had suddenly built one over a weekend.

I was delighted to have finished the school's layout so quickly, but I had no intention of rushing ours. Finishing it was becoming a moving target, and that was fine with me. For years, I had felt burdened by the work remaining; now, with so little left to do, I wanted to savor it. In any case, more remained than just a few details. Although I had been creating individual scenes specifically tailored to the camera, I still intended for the whole layout to have that "get it all at once" impact that is the hallmark of a good painting. I wanted an overall artistic effect, and it wasn't there—yet.

I asked Ellen to take a look. She had painted the buildings, signs, and figures, and she had mixed all the colors for the rocks—color that Dave Frary called the best he'd seen. But she wasn't part of the everyday work, and I hoped this would give her the perspective we needed. She took the same slow walk along the layout that Dave had when he was sizing it up for his photographs. Only instead of looking for vignettes and scenes, Ellen's aim was for a cohesive whole.

"I think it needs more green," she said finally. "In the front, here." She pointed to several areas, and I grabbed a bag of lichen and began spreading some around. I remembered that Dave had sprinkled some green in the foreground of some of *his* shots, and now Ellen was thinking the same way. The more she looked, the more she wanted to see green all across the front. With the reddish brown rocks beyond and the blue sky at the back, the effect would be of long horizontal bands of color rippling like the stripes of a banner.

Once I caught on, I asked Rolf to order two hundred trees and a dozen bags of ground cover. To make room for this great swath of green, we again called Bill, who by now must have been certain it was only a matter of time before he would be asked to cut through the walls so that we could extend the layout *beyond* the basement.

As the season wound down, we were almost as far from completion as we had been three months earlier. Rolf and I were delighted. Realizing that we were headed for another "last" season, Rolf decided that instead of installing Flextrak on our remaining stretch of mainline he would hand-lay the rails, and he began cutting wood for the individual ties. Work was expanding to fill the time available, and we had plenty of both.

Or did we? When I'm nearly finished with a painting, I know that if I let it drag on and enough time passes it will begin to reflect new ideas and enthusiasms, and before long it will morph into something altogether different. I didn't want that to happen with the layout; I didn't want to begin overhauling it from one end to the other. That would be too much work, and, besides, Ellen's suggestions had resolved the overall composition. So the next season was, truly, to be the last.

Rolf finished off Cielo Vista with a narrow gauge spur that appeared to connect with Judy's Loop and its quarry. Then he customized a gondola for wildflower excursions, fitting it with benches crowded with women and children. I responded by building a field of flowers and a knoll with an incomparable vista of the Dolores River. Rolf created a rickety gazebo to provide shade for the older women, and I arranged for two young Uncompahgre Utes to stage a mock fight on the cliff edge (the loser fell onto a mattress that was just out of sight). To endow the area with a sense of historical significance, we installed a monument, a tapered column resting on a stone plinth.

A visitor's first impression of the layout is that it's very long. Because you can't step back from it more than about ten feet, it fills your field of vision. An important aspect of the composition, however, is that the length is countered by elements that run directly *into* the layout: the ravine, the canyon at the mine, the Dolores River. These act like verticals in a long painting, subdividing the space and slowing up the eye as it speeds from one side to the other. (They also act subliminally as obstacles for the trains, making them seem to work hard as they force their way through the landscape.)

I decided to add another perpendicular element: a road that would cut across into the layout at its narrowest point. I wanted, almost as a game, to see how much illusion of depth I could get in the available space, which was about four feet. I started by designing a couple of buildings for the immediate foreground, using color and texture to make them seem close. One was painted schoolbus yellow, and the other was a log cabin that Rolf made from actual twigs. The train was crossing a trestle behind the buildings, and beyond the train came a ridge with a tiny road zigzagging up it. Placed on top of the ridge was a cluster of Monopoly-sized houses plus a factory. The final layer was the backdrop, on which was painted more mountains and the sky. Through the camera's lens, from the log cabin to the miniature town looked to be at least five miles.

As spring approached, Rolf was finishing up the section of hand-laid track. The year before, we had talked of throwing a party to commemorate the driving of our golden spike, but now we wanted to avoid anything so final. We just didn't want to say, "It's finished." Then one day I saw that everything on our list had been done. It was as if we had crossed the equator but never felt a bump. Rolf packed up his tools.

Nevertheless, I didn't think I would know if it was over, for sure, until November. For sixteen years, November's cold weather and proximity to Christmas had reawakened my interest in the layout and lured me back into the basement.

November came. I was busy with architecture, but I went down to the basement for a look around. In other years part of the layout had always been unfinished, and the sight of bare plywood or some roughed-in blue foam had started my juices flowing. But now I saw what I had seen the previous spring, and I was happy to leave it exactly as it was. To protect the layout from dust and from people inadvertently banging into it, Bill Berry hung sheets of Plexiglas across the front, encasing it like a museum diorama.

In the ensuing weeks, I heard myself telling people that, yes, the layout *was* finished. I would explain that it had been a project, not a hobby, and that the project was over. The reaction was often skeptical: "Oh, you'll never stop working on that thing—you'll see."

⸻

They were right. True, two years went by with no further layout work, but all at once I found myself on the phone to *Model Railroader,* proposing an article that would be called "The Magic of Illusion." I hadn't started the layout's center section when Dave Frary had made his visit, and it contained the work I had composed, deliberately, with photography in mind. That those photographs had never been taken seemed to me to be unfinished business.

I planned for a diagram to accompany each picture, illustrating the basic visual mechanics of the scene. The view up the road was just one of a half dozen locations where I had employed formal devices for expanding the sense of space.

When the magazine agreed to send Dave, Rolf came over to dust off the rivers, stand up a few men that had fallen down on the job, and wreck a locomotive. (I wanted one photograph to show that "space" could be thought of as an interval of time, and a wrecked locomotive created a moment—the moment of the crash—that had clearly occurred before the picture was taken.)

The flurry of photography did not, however, mean we were back working on the layout. When people asked if it was finished, I still said yes. But to myself, I would add, "At least for now."

PART TWO

FOUNTAIN OF YOUTH

What struck me most vividly when I thought the layout might be finished was how much enthusiasm—and curiosity—I still felt for model railroading as a hobby. Just because I was no longer building a layout myself didn't mean I stopped reading the magazines. I found I wanted to get behind the scenes, to see some of the top layouts firsthand and meet the people who had built them. "They'll all be geeks and nerds," a friend said to me, and while I didn't know if I would agree, I was certain of one thing: they inhabited a world that fascinated me.

My first stop: Milwaukee, model railroading's unquestioned capital. Milwaukee is the home of the W. K. Walthers Company and Kalmbach Publishing, the twin pillars upon which the hobby of HO model railroading rests. I planned to visit both companies because I wanted a basic idea of how the $400 million business of model railroading worked—what made it tick.

I arrived at Walthers on a rainy morning. When I turned into the parking lot, the pavement was a shiny black, the long, low building a dull white. A half dozen women stood smoking cigarettes, protected by a concrete overhang. Above the overhang, and partly blocked by it, was a large billboard with a drawing of a locomotive.

It is virtually impossible to build an HO layout without dealing with Walthers, which is the country's largest wholesale distributor of model railroad products. Hobbyists buy from any of the 3,500 dealers associated with Walthers, or direct from the company's Web site or their annual catalogs. They print three separate catalogs. One is for the smaller scales, one for the bigger scales, and one for HO, which is by far the largest. Costing $22.95, it has more than one thousand pages and lists eighty thousand items. I had bought the latest edition every year since Rolf had come to work, and few days had gone by that we hadn't paged through it looking for stuff we needed.

The company got its start in 1932 with a catalog published by Bill Walthers, a forty-year-old electrical engineer. Expensive for the time at $3, it featured designs of electrical control systems for switches and signals that Walthers had developed on a layout he built in his attic. Sales in the first year totaled just $500, but business picked up when Walthers realized that instead of offering a design, he could sell the thing itself, ready-made. He soon expanded his product line to include locomotives, rolling stock, and decals. In the hobby's boom years right after World War II, Walthers employed sixty people.

Bill Walthers retired in the late 1950s, turning control of the company over to his son Bruce. These were tough times for the business. The golden age of the railroads had ended, many of

Walthers's products were out of date, and the slot car craze was just around the corner. From Walthers's perspective, slot cars weren't just another toy. They had the same kinetics as model trains. They ran by remote control (which Joshua Cowen believed was central to the appeal of model railroads), and they offered two things trains did not: flashy speed and head-to-head racing. The pace of life was quickening, and slot cars made toy trains seem old-fashioned.

Wholesalers began dropping Walthers's products, making room on their shelves for the cars. Bruce Walthers responded by becoming a wholesaler himself. He started including the products of other companies in his catalog, mostly those of low-volume mom-and-pop operations that were happy to accept modest profits in exchange for the chance to make a living out of what was for them essentially a hobby. This left room for Walthers to mark up items while still keeping costs within range of his customers. The 1970s saw the catalog growing fast, and in the 1980s Walthers began to carry foreign lines, including Märklin, which was the Lionel of Europe. Meanwhile, the much feared slot cars came and went, never posing a serious threat to model railroading. Like the remote control cars and planes that followed them, slot cars lacked staying power. They didn't involve commitment to a long-term project and many required big tracks at "parlors," many of which soon went broke.

At Walthers, business grew, but now a new kind of competition appeared—computer games. The popularity of the games produced by companies such as Nintendo and Atari is linked to our shift from the mechanical age to the electronic, and it isn't going away. But, so far, no damage has been done to Walthers's bottom line thanks to renewed interest in railroading among older hobbyists. In fact, in the last twelve years, the company's sales have doubled.

"It's the fountain of youth," John Sanheim, vice president of marketing and sales, told me as we sat in his office. "We're not talking about kids here; these are men in their midfifties, men playing with the same toys they had as kids.

"Model railroading," John continued, "encompasses more than the trains themselves. It's a real skill. Track planning. Construction. It's things you do with your hands."

Fountain of youth. Men playing with toys. Using your hands. I nodded and took notes, but I was distracted by the thought that I had been on Walthers's radar screen all along, just another guy moving through his fifties, buying stuff tracked by their database.

"There are fewer people in the hobby today than ten years ago," John said, "but they spend more and live longer." He added that layouts are bigger because people have more space. "Most of our sales," he said, "come from the rust belt—Pennsylvania, Ohio, Indiana, Michigan, and here in Wisconsin. The houses have heated basements, and of course the winters are long."

John described the business as "incredibly seasonal. We'll have just one ad in the August issue of *Model Railroader* but ten in October when we're putting on the push for Christmas. There's no action in the summer because modelers tend to be family men who do things outdoors with their kids." During periods of recession, sales stay strong. "Guys get laid off," John said, "and then they have more time for their trains.

"At any time," he continued, "what sells best are the locomotives. Then cars, then track. Scenery comes last. A lot of people never get around to scenery. In fact, some never get around to running their trains at all. They just collect them. We've even got customers who collect *kits*—with no intention of ever putting them together." Walthers sells equipment for all scales, but 75 percent of their gross is HO. "The other scales come and go," John said, "and right now the bigger sizes are popular. But HO is always there." In 2001, Walthers sold a total of 129 miles of HO track. That's 11,223 scale miles—almost forty Nullarbor Straights, and enough track to stretch almost halfway around the earth at the equator.

Manufacturers have created a universe of accessories. Take figures. The catalog offers model Arabs, riot police, wedding groups, elderly people being pushed in wheelchairs, sunbathers, tennis players. You can buy Adam and Eve being expelled from Eden, or a cheery Tyrolean band. A big chunk of the catalog— sixty-one pages—is devoted to the military, while circus items fill thirteen.

John has been with Walthers for twenty-eight years, and as he showed me around the plant, he tossed out statistics without breaking stride. The building was 112,000 square feet, and it was one of twelve GEXs (government exchanges, a sort of civilian PX) erected around the country in the early 1960s. The company has 150 employees. Here was the catalog department, the graphics department, the computer department. The people I was meeting were relaxed and welcoming. The walls were covered with photographs and paintings of trains—even the bathroom, I would find out, had the railroad motif.

John introduced me to Bill Wischer, head of new product development. Bill's department was cluttered like the room of a kid with indulgent parents. Every surface was piled with books and models, every wall was papered with drawings and photographs. Designers sat in front of computer screens in workspaces that were nominally their own, but which were actually part of a continuum of clutter. Bill himself was built compactly, as if designed not to take up any more of the department's space than necessary.

One third of Walthers's gross sales (and a larger percentage of its net), he told me, comes from its own products. What the company chooses to make, or not to make, can quickly establish trends within the hobby. In the early 1980s, for example, modelers who wanted authentic-looking tracks had no choice but to lay their own, by hand—work which only a dedicated few were willing to undertake. Then Walthers introduced track, mass-produced, that looked just as good as hand-laid. With this new track, casual modelers began to reach for higher levels of realism in other areas, too, especially structures. They didn't have the time or inclination to build the models themselves, however, so for 1999, Bill Wischer's department produced kits that came prepainted, with the windows, doors, and architectural detailing already in place. All the customer did was snap the walls together—no gluing. In 2001, another step: Walthers began offering fully assembled structures. The modeler now merely removed his water tower (or his sawmill, or his brewery) from the box and placed it on his layout. Walthers even began making structures that, like my old Lionel log loader, *did* things: the catalog offered a drive-in restaurant, circa 1955, with flashing neon lights, and Bill showed me a prototype movie theater with electroluminescent lights scrolling along the marquee; both models were part of a new series Walthers was calling "action" structures.

The locomotive remains the modeler's core purchase and the hobby's biggest profit center. Over the last ten years, the leading locomotive manufacturers (Life-Like, Atlas, Bachmann, Rivarossi, Athearn, and Walthers themselves) have offered increasingly detailed products, and a wider range, to take advantage of the trend toward realism. (Rivarossi, for example, currently has fifty different steam engines in production.) Now the hobbyist can buy a roster of authentic locomotives for most any major railroad he chooses to model.

With this frenzy for authenticity, something obvious was missing: sound. A few diesel locomotives came with sound, but model steam engines just hummed along the tracks, unaccompanied by the escaping steam and thrashing drivers that made the real thing so thrilling. Companies building the larger-scale loco-motives had begun to offer sound, but the systems were still too big to shoehorn into a six-inch-long HO engine. Elite modelers who understood electronics had managed to install customized units, but no one had figured out how to offer one for sale at a reasonable price. Now Bill Wischer led me to his test track, which was an oval laid out on a sturdy gray table. He slid a steam locomotive out of a box and placed it on the tracks.

Sssis. Thunk. Shhhhhuuh . . . The locomotive sat there, not moving, making the heavy popping and hissing sounds of an idling steam engine. The whistle blew. With the chugging ex-haust synchronized to the speed of the engine and the bell clang-ing, the locomotive pulled away. Bill handed me the box, which had an art deco look to the lettering and graphics. Broadway Limited Imports, it said—a new company, selling *sound,* retail, for about $280. Someone would later say to me: "If you have twenty locomotives, and you buy one of these, you now have one locomotive—you'll never run anything else." (That night I called Rolf to describe what I had seen. He told me he had ten on order but hadn't been able to get even one; they were all sold out.)

Fully assembled structures. Sound. Here were two directions for the hobby that spelled good news for Walthers's bottom line. A third was China. Over lunch, Bill told me that beginning in the late 1980s the Chinese had been building more and more of the Walthers line. Bill averages four trips a year to Beijing. "Typ-ically, our work is done by young girls in their twenties, straight from the farm. It's strange," he said, "to see one of those girls making a diesel locomotive you know is going to wind up in the hands of some fifty-five-year-old American who has no idea where it came from."

Bill has been with Walthers for twenty-two years. "It's a business of onesies and twosies," he told me back at the plant as we walked past row after row of shelves in the warehouse. More than twenty employees were roaming the aisles looking for inventory numbers matching those on the order forms. They collected items in baskets that trundled along a conveyor belt to the shipping area. The mood in the warehouse was calm and detached. A $150 Kato SD90/43 MAC diesel with a five-pole motor, dual brass flywheels, LED headlights, printed number boards, windshield lights, and separate MU hoses may cause its new owner to become slightly giddy with excitement as he removes it from the box, but in the warehouse it's only a catalog number. Bill picked up an order form. Ten items were listed, most just once. "Some of the things are ordered so infrequently we sell maybe one of them a year," he said, shrugging, "and we probably have ten thousand items that basically never sell at all."

At most companies, an executive would check inventory and if he saw that not a single #704-9316 (an $8.99 replacement filter for an airbrush cleaner) had been sold for three years, he would discontinue it. But Walthers doesn't think that way. The company sees a sixty-five-year-old modeler who has decided to weather his new Pullman-Standard single-door auto parts boxcar and discovers that his twenty-year-old airbrush is clogged. Gotta have that filter. And he has to get it quickly, or his enthusiasm for the project may wane. Which would be bad for the hobby. Which would be bad for Walthers.

Just as important as stocking obscure items is keeping things cheap. Model railroading took off in the Depression, and cheapness is in its DNA. John Allen once estimated that his expenses, per day, were equal to the cost of two packs of cigarettes. Bill McClanahan's *Scenery for Model Railroads* (first published in 1958) is a paean to inventiveness, goading the modeler to make trees from sponges and steel wool, ground cover from dyed saw-dust, and reeds from broom straws. Another book lists sixteen basic tools required to make scenery, and the most expensive is a staple gun. Most issues of *Model Railroader* feature projects such as constructing a coaling tower out of a piece of PVC pipe or a mine from shirt cardboard. They print diagrams of layouts that squeeze into closets and onto the tops of coffee tables. In "Model of the Month" you will see a scratch-built freight car, breathtak-ingly detailed, that took perhaps six months to create—but cost less than $20. The message is clear: this is an egalitarian hobby in which skill and patience count far more than money does.

Lately, however, there have been signs that the baby boomers are trying to buy their way in. Walthers's fully assembled struc-tures ($30 to $40) are selling briskly. Injection-molded rock cliffs, like those it once took Bill McClanahan so long to build, are available for $45. You can buy a junkyard or a cemetery for $27. Forty dollars brings a fully assembled firehouse right to your door. Trees? You can have a six-inch acacia for $12, a grove of ten sycamores for $150. Pros such as Rolf are in demand, whether to work alongside the owner (as he did with me) or to build entire custom layouts from the ground up. To the old-time modeler, it must seem as if the barbarians are pulling into the station.

My other stop was at Kalmbach Publishing, in Waukesha, a sprawling Milwaukee suburb. Kalmbach owns *Model Railroader,* whose editorial offices are located in a modern building elegantly finished in chrome and glass. (Kalmbach also prints *Classic Toy Trains* and *Garden Railways,* as well as magazines not related to trains, such as *Bead and Button, Birder's World,* and *Dollhouse Miniatures*—fourteen titles in all.)

Walthers's shelves contain the raw material, while *Model*

Railroader, with a circulation hovering around two hundred thousand, is the hobby's cheerleader. Other model railroading magazines (about a dozen are published) are available by subscription or in hobby stores, but *Model Railroader* is the one seen on newsstands, its bright, graphic covers attracting newcomers as pollen attracts bees. The magazine's brief is to inspire and inform; it prints articles like "The ABCs of Painting and Lettering" and "How to Paint a Wabash Caboose," along with scale drawings of everything from laundry to Lincoln's funeral train. New products are reviewed and locomotives track-tested (the data panel is detailed enough to make you think you have stumbled into the pages of *Road & Track* or *Consumer Reports*). The message, repeated in issue after issue, is empowering: you can do this; you can have a layout that looks like the layouts we publish.

It worked for me.

RULING AN EMPIRE

While I was in Milwaukee, *Model Railroader*'s senior editor Jim Hediger invited me to visit his layout. Jim has been with the magazine for thirty years and has seen as many layouts as anyone. "I like that we all start with the same stuff and wind up with different things," he told me. He had picked me up at my hotel, arriving exactly on time, and now we were headed west in his Dodge minivan. Suburban Milwaukee was giving way to county roads.

Jim is in his sixties. A big man, he drove steadily, deliberately, his hands relaxed on the wheel. Our conversation stuck mostly to technical subjects. Along the way, the Dodge thumped over three sets of tracks. Each belonged to a different railroad, which Jim spoke of as if it were an old friend.

His ancestors were Swiss; some manufactured cigars, others served in the papal guards. His parents both worked for the Detroit, Toledo, and Ironton Railroad. Their only child, he was eight when they gave him his first model trains. "American Flyer," he said. "It couldn't be Lionel because of my parents being railroaders; the third rail was unacceptable to them."

I had come to realize that visiting a layout is a surprisingly intrusive act. Consider my morning with Jim. Except for a couple of brief encounters at the office, I was a stranger to him. Yet he drove me into his neighborhood, brought me to his house, and led me down into his basement, where he was soon showing me how one of his staging yards cantilevered over his washing machine. I was seeing how Jim Hediger lived. But the layout itself would be the most revealing. For the experienced modeler— which I now proudly considered myself to be—another person's layout is full of clues.

I had discovered this a few months before, in a basement near home.

"I have been very sick," Ned Swigart had told me on the phone. He said he was being kept alive by a lot of drugs and an experimental heart pump more powerful than a conventional pacemaker. He mentioned the second article about my layout that had run in *Model Railroader,* and asked if I would help refine a layout that had been built for him in Denver and recently delivered. I was flattered by the thought of being an adviser, but I would have gone to see Ned Swigart anyway.

Mr. Swigart had been my biology teacher at the Gunnery, a small boarding school in Washington, Connecticut, and I had not seen him in forty years. He owned a layout back then, too, and he had persuaded the school's headmaster to sanction the

Model Railroad Club, which allowed a lucky few of us to escape from the campus for an occasional evening in the Swigart basement. Mrs. Swigart, I recall, supplied chocolate chip cookies.

I admired Mr. Swigart. He was a robust outdoorsman who really lived for the subject he taught, and he never talked down to us. He was an imaginative teacher who often took an unorthodox approach to get his point across. Luckily for me, he applied some of this creativity to my final grade. The scores of my quizzes and written work pointed implacably to an *F,* but I had made an anatomical drawing of a pigeon (on a windowshade, so it could be pulled down for display) that he used in his classes, and he said anyone who could draw a pigeon that well deserved to pass biology.

As a teenager, I had wanted to be enthusiastic about his layout, which was inspired by the Old West, but it was so cluttered that instead of evoking wide-open spaces it looked urban. Tracks ran everywhere and buildings occupied what little space was left over. In my senior year, at Mr. Swigart's invitation, I painted a backdrop. Copied from a photograph of Yosemite, the idea was to create a big, open vista that would be an antidote to the foreground congestion. Unwittingly, I used untreated Masonite, which absorbed the pigment. Within a month, my greens and blues turned brown, and Angel Falls went from white to tan. Yosemite had become Cleveland. But that original layout was long gone, and I was looking forward to seeing its successor.

I drove up through the woods to the Swigarts' house. The Cape Cod character I remembered had been diluted by several additions. I wondered if Ned, too, would be different from how I remembered him, but as he strode onto the porch to greet me, I saw the same tall, broad-shouldered man with the quick grin and thick, round glasses. But sitting in his study, he told me his energy had to be rationed and that he needed a nap every three hours "to recharge." He then proceeded to talk nonstop with such intensity that I worried he wouldn't last even the three hours.

"I've always been a dreamer," he said, "and I've lived much of my life in my imagination. When I was younger, the main reason for the model trains was that they allowed me to think about places and get excited about things I loved but didn't have time for, and now that I can't get around so well, the new layout is letting me dream that same way again."

We had talked for an hour before he led me to the narrow basement stairs. At the bottom, he stepped aside, revealing a layout that looked eerily similar to the one I remembered from forty years before. It was again L-shaped and supported on a spindly network of wooden legs. In his exuberance, Ned had used five different scales, and he was proudly calling this confusion "forced perspective." A piece of ground a foot square was supposed to be a prairie; it was covered with a herd of buffalo. All four seasons and two eras, the 1890s and the 1930s, were represented. Scenes jostled for supremacy; as much was going on here as in our layout, which was ten times bigger.

I was afraid Ned would sense my dismay, but he was busy adding a couple of last-minute questions to a list he had fastened to a clipboard. Should there be more conifers along the ridge? Where could the Indian canoe go? Could the bathing pool in the stream be enlarged? How could he keep the figures from falling over? How far apart should the telegraph poles be placed? Where should the church go?

He said more figures were on order and that a relative was coming next week to install additional lights in the buildings. He hoped to settle, soon, on the location of a promontory where he could place a bugling moose. Dozens of trees awaited planting, and lest any open ground be visible, it could be covered, instantly, by grabbing for one of the backup buildings scattered through-out the basement on tables and shelves. I had wondered if Ned, in view of his health, might be racing to finish the layout. In-stead, he told me he was looking for ways to expand it. "I never want it to be finished," he said.

I began to appreciate details that I hadn't noticed at first. The layout's builder had carved the rocks from plaster, infusing them with his firsthand knowledge of local Colorado geology. Ned's buildings were equally satisfying. They not only looked old, they *were* old, many of them dating back to his previous layout. The interiors were crowded with furniture and figures: a pool game was in progress in the saloon, a maid was making beds in the hotel, a side of beef hung from a chain in a butcher shop. In order for the visitor to see inside the buildings, Ned had removed the roofs. He is an expert on Indian culture, and his numerous Indian scenes were crammed with authentic details. You needed to rev up your imagination to make all this work, but the effort was worth it.

I didn't leave until well past the three-hour deadline. As I drove away, Ned was already back in the house, doubtless headed to his bedroom, where, while he napped, he would dream of fresh ways to make his layout still more complicated.

At Jim Hediger's, we went right downstairs. The ride out from the hotel had been the equivalent of the chat Ned and I had be-fore viewing his layout. This preamble, I would learn as I visited other modelers, was part of the etiquette of the hobby. (The hos-pitable atmosphere also made it particularly rude to say anything critical about the layout, even if you wanted to.)

Like John Allen's house, Jim's (a trim, unassuming ranch) was cut into a steeply sloping bank, and the stairs led down to a den with windows and a door to the outside. The layout room was adjacent to the den, and my first impression as I stepped into it was of acute claustrophobia. The tracks were on two levels, one about counter height, the other at shoulder height, and they ran not only around the walls but also out into the center of the room, on a peninsula. Scenery blocked any chance to see for more than a few feet; I felt as if I had entered the stacks of a library. Unlike Ned Swigart's layout, which was an object, this was an *environment,* and I couldn't find anywhere to stand that would allow me to take in the whole thing at once. You viewed small sections, then moved along narrow aisles to look at other places. You saw the scenery as a series of vignettes, just as you would experience it as you looked out the window of an actual train.

The layout had been conceived as an arrangement of yards, industries, sidings, and main lines that enabled Jim to run his trains in a way that simulated the day-to-day operations of a real railroad. My trains go around and around; his travel from one place to another—what is called "point-to-point." Hobbyists have understood this essential difference from the beginning, but since model railroading traces its ancestry back to the circle under the Christmas tree, not to the real thing, the tradition of trains running in circles is hard to break. Even John Allen's layout was, schematically, a circle.

Early efforts at point-to-point were on small layouts, and trains could run only a few seconds before they reached the end of the line. In the 1970s, however, model railroads began to grow, and at the same time hobbyists became increasingly attracted to modeling historically correct prototypes. Interest in point-to-point was renewed; still, modelers were frustrated by train rooms that weren't *quite* big enough.

Enter John Armstrong. *Model Railroader* billed him as "the

dean of track planning," and his diagrams were frequently published as a way of helping rookie modelers start off on the right foot. A Purdue graduate and former mechanical engineer in naval ordnance research and development, Armstrong relished devising unusual ways to cram a lot of track into small spaces. Over the years, he drew plans for every imaginable type of layout, including one that fit on a Murphy bed. In addition, he developed his own lexicon of terms, such as "dual aisle way no-stoop" (a layout you need not duck under to reach the controls), "dog bone" (a narrow layout that flares at the ends), and "double-faced backdrop" (the backdrop is in the center, with the trains running around it). Confronted with the task of concocting hundreds of place-names for his diagrams, he came up with such beauties as Pine Not, Jock's Trap, Bee Falls, Llawn Mawr, and Desmaigne Yard. For Anglophiles, he drew a plan with towns called Tyllywymbledon Junction, Blicester, and Worpington Halt. Armstrong was captivated by the relationship between a model railroad and the space it occupied, which eventually led him to propose the double-deck configuration. And Jim Hediger became one of the first to try it out.

He began by experimenting with the basic elements. What heights should the decks be? What depth? How would the trains get from one deck to another? How would the decks be supported? Eager and inventive, Jim spent eighteen months tinkering with ideas before he was ready to begin. These were exciting times: Jim Hediger, the unassuming former schoolteacher, was not only building a large layout, he was working with a layout type that was highly unusual—even pioneering. The railroad prototype on which it was based had been an easy choice: the Detroit, Toledo, and Ironton, which his parents had worked for. He chose a segment that ran through southern Ohio, and with characteristic directness, he named his railroad the Ohio Southern.

Eight years later, with the layout nearly finished, Jim received news that was right out of Kafka: the city sewer line was being rebuilt—and, incredibly, it ran directly under his house. Years of his work would have to be ripped out. Jim somehow managed to convince himself that being forced to replace 80 percent of his layout was actually a good thing, an opportunity, even, to eliminate some of the weaknesses of his original plan. What he had no intention of changing was the basic double-deck setup. That was a great success. Articles that Jim had written about the layout had twice been printed by *Model Railroader,* bringing him a degree of fame. The twin decks limited the possibilities for scenery (the lower level was little more than a shelf), but that was just fine with Jim and many other modelers for whom scenery had never been the top priority.

The satisfactions of operating trains on a point-to-point layout included sharing the experience with eight to ten friends, who would meet for "operating sessions." Transformers and power packs had become obsolete; new handheld devices resembling TV remotes enabled each locomotive to be run independent of the others; an operator walked along the aisles adjusting the speed of his train to fit the situation. Each train had its own assignment. One hauled coal. Another stopped at the various industries. Express passenger trains rushed down the main line while switch engines poked around in the staging yards assembling trains. Coordinating all this was the dispatcher, an imperial figure who spent the session seated in front of the master control panel. The dispatcher was, of course, the layout's owner.

In building the scenery for our layout, I had edited and compressed the landscape; in building his operating layout, Jim edited and compressed the way a railroad runs. I had immersed myself in William Henry Jackson's landscape vistas, while Jim had studied timetables, crew changes, interchange traffic, the output of industries, trackage rights, and the ability of locomotives to haul long strings of freight cars up grades.

He had more than one hundred locomotives and six hundred cars. Trains climbed from one level to another by spiraling around and around in a helix, which was a drum five feet in diameter. Jim showed me his seven towns, four staging yards (total capacity: twenty-six complete trains), and a dozen industries. He pointed out surveillance cameras that allowed him to keep track of the trains on a split-screen monitor located in his dispatcher's alcove. He ran an eight-foot-long coal train from one end of the layout to the other, winding along the lower level, then through the three laps of the helix, finally onto the upper level. Total time for the trip: ten minutes.

Here was a modest man, living in a modest house, ruling an empire.

Tony Koester ("pronounced Custer, like the general," he had told me over the phone) suggested we meet at McDonald's so that he could lead me along the back roads to his house. This was Newton, in northern New Jersey, a wooded area that looks rural until you realize that the canopy of trees conceals a suburban landscape with many houses and an intricate system of roads. I was happy to trail Tony's Audi A4, a five-speed stick shift that he drives fast, and not have to worry about getting lost.

It was a warm day in early fall. The sky was gray, and the first yellow was coming into the leaves. Back at McDonald's, Tony had told me exactly where to park when I pulled into his driveway, and now, as we made our way past masons who were rebuilding the terrace in front of his house, he even pointed out just where I should step.

Once inside the front hall, I saw a print of a railroad painting, but that was the only visible artifact of his passion for trains. In the living room, the walls were filled with photographs Tony and his wife, Judy, had taken on their numerous trips abroad. The room's cathedral ceiling and dark wood beams made it feel like an extension of the forest outside. Tony motioned for me to sit on the sofa and presented me with a gift: a hopper car from his recently dismantled railroad, the Allegheny Midland.

Tony is six-two and, like Jim Hediger, he's in his early sixties. Were it not for his white hair, I would have guessed he was ten years younger. He wears V-neck sweaters and large glasses with a light brown tint to the lenses. He has the look of a professor who is pleased but surprised that a student has just given a good answer. He holds a degree in electrical engineering from Purdue and worked from 1981 until recently in the telecommunications business, first for Bell Laboratories (AT&T's research arm) and then, when Bell was split up, for Bell Communications Research (later Telcordia Technologies), which developed the software for toll-free calling and caller ID.

The engineering degree, the high-tech job in suburban New Jersey, and his extensive travels (including, recently, a trip to China) suggest someone for whom model railroading would be, at most, a casual hobby. But Tony is dead serious about it. He holds deep convictions about what model railroading can and should be. And he is full of propaganda for his cause, a latter-day Joshua Lionel Cowen.

"I have a mission, a vision," he told me without a trace of embarrassment. The mission hadn't defined itself until Tony was in his thirties, but trains as something special entered his life early.

The eldest of three children, he was born in Hampton, Iowa, about fifty-five miles north of Des Moines. He was two when his father ordered trains from Lionel for Christmas. As the big day approached, Tony's father made trip after trip to the post office. No trains. Finally, they arrived—on the day before Christmas. The postmaster, aware of how important the package was, delivered it himself.

Father and son were soon improving the stock Lionel equipment, cutting corrugated cardboard into strips to add extra ties to the tracks and disguising the third rail. During high school, however, the trains were shelved. "I did the girls, cars, sports thing," he said to me. He settled down early, marrying Judy when he was just eighteen. Trains came back into his life when he enrolled at Purdue and became a member of the school's model railroad club. The club had a distinguished alumnus: John Armstrong—the same John Armstrong *Model Railroader* called "the dean of track planning."

After Purdue, Tony worked as a surveyor, but his interest in trains led him to visit the offices of a magazine called *Railroad Model Craftsman,* where he was offered a job. He stayed for twelve years, becoming the editor along the way. Representing the magazine at a convention, he befriended a man named Allen McClelland. McClelland's layout was a point-to-point, and he soon had Tony persuaded that this was the way to go.

Tony began designing a layout that would connect, hypothetically, with his new friend's. While Allen had modeled a line that ran through Virginia, Tony's would continue north through West Virginia; he would call it the Allegheny Midland. One of the first second-generation modelers, he was able to rely on techniques the older men had struggled to develop. He was committed to a major layout (twenty-four by twenty-nine feet, with extensions into adjacent rooms), and he was competing with both the Armstrong legacy and McClelland's existing layout. "I knew it had to be good," Tony told me.

I first saw pictures of the Allegheny Midland about the time I began to build the scenery for our layout. John Allen's shots had been highly realistic, but something invariably betrayed the fact that they were of a model railroad. With Tony's you just could not be sure. His black-and-white shots were particularly convincing. You'd see a large, black steam locomotive pulling an endless line of black hopper cars along a straight that extended off both sides of the picture, suggesting a main line of great length. Invariably, the train would be passing a structure modeled from real life, a paper company or a freight house or a loading dock. The background was an anonymous stretch of the Allegheny Mountains, made up of thousands of what Tony called "puffball trees," which he fashioned from polyfiber at the rate of one every thirty seconds. (By contrast, my handmade pines had taken forty-five minutes apiece.) It was always a day in the late 1950s, around noon, with a flat, featureless sky. This was a time when diesels had replaced steam engines, except in places like the Alleghenies, where coal was plentiful and cheap. Tony's diesels served as a reminder that the days of steam were numbered, and this invested his roster of steam locomotives with particular poignancy. His photographs were devoid of optical tricks, and the stories they told were tied to authentic aspects of prototype railroading, especially the unglamorous business of moving coal through the poverty of Appalachia. The coal was heavy, the grades steep, the engines grimy and muscular. Tony refrained from puns or cute names. Other men had pointed the way, but when Tony built his Allegheny Midland, model railroading finally found a place to operate out from under the shadow of the Christmas tree.

The layout's gritty realism caught the eye, but its staying power came from the way it ran. Thanks to the point-to-point configuration, Tony, like Jim Hediger, could simulate the operations of a real railroad. During the operating sessions, Tony encouraged the use of authentic railroading terms. Leaving cars at an industry was called "spotting" or "setting out." When you added an extra engine, you were "cutting it in," in order to "double the hill." An on-time arrival was "on the advertised." He assigned operators to trains or to switching duties in one of the yards. A new timetable was published for each session. Operators kept track of time by referring to a clock that ran at five times normal speed. The "fast clock," as it was called, compensated for the unrealistically short distances (just a few feet) between towns.

The operators walked beside the trains using handheld radio-controlled throttles, to adjust their locomotives' speed. But the dispatcher (Tony) made the important decisions, such as when their trains should move and what routing they should use. He issued his orders in the metronomic cadences of a real dispatcher: "E-N-G-I-N-E-F-I-F-T-Y-N-I-N-E . . ." He took remote control to a new level: Tony now controlled his locomotives through his friends. At the height of the action the railroad jargon was so thick that it sounded like a foreign language.

Even though Tony lived hundreds of miles away from Allen McClelland, they would operate their two railroads as one. For example, a train would set off from the north end of Tony's line, run through the layout, and when it reached the yards at the south end, he would call Allen, who would then dispatch an identical train to run north to south on his layout. If the train was delayed on Tony's layout and "arrived" on Allen's behind schedule, its operator might find that he had to buck a series of northbound locals that were now entitled to use the main line.

"The Allegheny Midland became an institution," Tony told me. Over the years, thousands of modelers made the pilgrimage to Newton, and the layout was the subject of a commercial video. But mostly, the word spread because of Tony himself. Tony wrote beautifully, and the thing he wrote best and most often about was his own railroad. Not long after he left *Railroad Model Craftsman* he was hired by *Model Railroader* to write a monthly column called "Trains of Thought." The column was a pulpit, and the subjects of the sermons were the manifold joys, the purity, and the sheer righteousness of operation. To Tony, you were either an operator and loved operation or you were cast into the netherworld of the scenery makers, doomed to wander the earth as a lost soul. Columns addressed such questions as How long is a passing track? How much should cars weigh? and Is free ballast really free? Subtexts provided wisdom about truck screw tension and cast frogs for code 55 turnouts. Tony preached directly to the brethren, making the assumption that readers were familiar with his Allegheny Midland, and that, for example, references to the layout's towns—Alta-pass, Big Springs Junction, Otter Creek—could parachute into the text without any need of explanation.

I loved the column. Despite the pedagogical bent, its tone was light and self-deprecating. ("Some of us admit right up front we're playing with toys—and are quite pleased about it to boot.") His style was vivid and jaunty; for example, "Plug in the vacuum cleaner" was his code for a crash. His mine of subjects was bottomless, and you knew he knew what he was talking about. The real clincher was his conviction. He could lure you into buying a corny line like "I feel a warm glow when the railroad comes alive during a well-executed operating session."

By the late 1990s, however, the Allegheny Midland had been finished for more than twenty years; Tony the businessman described it as "fully amortized." In the latest operating layouts—and the success of the Allegheny Midland had inspired many—train crews now made more of their own decisions (as they do in real life), and the dispatcher's role was deemphasized. The Allegheny Midland was dated.

"I knew it was time to dismantle the layout the same way a flight instructor knows when his student can solo," Tony (who is a flight instructor) told me. He was close to retirement at Telcordia, a move that would give him the time he needed to start from scratch on an all-new layout, whose construction he would be describing in a series of articles for *Model Railroader*. Years before, he had been proud that his job at *Railroad Model Craftsman* had paid for his house (he would tell his kids, "This is the house that model railroading built"); now model railroading would be paying, in part, for his retirement.

Tony wanted to show me where the new layout was going to be, and I followed him to the basement. Even though I knew better, I half expected that his old Allegheny Midland, which was so vivid in my mind, would still be there. Instead, I saw bare shelves, a few tracks in a yard, and piles of boxes. It was an interstitial moment for Tony. His old layout was gone, and the new one hadn't been started to take its place.

He handed me a white foam-core model, a little bigger than a shoe box, which showed how his new layout would be fitted into the basement. Double-decker shelves would run along the walls, with the objective being to fit the maximum amount of track into the space.

"The old layout was all on one level," he said, striding around, "and its main line was only two hundred feet long." He gestured to the wall that separated the train room from the garage. "I'm moving this," he said, "and with the extra area—plus of course the second deck—the new plan gives me five hundred feet of main line. That's eight scale miles," he added, not waiting for me to do the math.

Tony's family had moved from Iowa to Indiana when he was nine, in time for him to experience the last four years that steam engines were used on the Nickel Plate Road. The Nickel Plate's route stretched from Buffalo to Chicago, and its big locomotives and high-speed service gripped Tony's imagination. In fact, Nickel Plate rolling stock had frequently surfaced on the Allegheny Midland. At Walthers, John Sanheim had called model railroading the fountain of youth, and now Tony was turning to his childhood for inspiration. The execution of the new layout, however, would be a proving ground for the theories of a grown-up.

"A layout needs a logical reason for existence" was a Koester axiom; now he was building the framework of that logic, selecting that part of the Nickel Plate line that could be abstracted most successfully into model form. Track planner John Armstrong had concentrated on the relationship between the configuration of a layout and the space it occupied; Tony's elegant variation on that theme called for "the wonderful excitement of a prototype fitting the circumstance of a layout." Tony's process was one of reduction, of gradually paring down possibilities until he was left with choices that could not be questioned.

"I want to get as close as possible to reality," he said, "and the prototype defines that reality." He called the prototype his benchmark, and like a bloodhound he sniffed out details of the Nickel Plate. Using books, interviews, and field trips to photograph and measure existing structures he assembled his facts. "Field trips are fun," he said. "I love the old industries, the cranky stuff." Nothing was so sweet as the prospect of a visitor challenging the correctness of the pitch of a roof or the number

In the 1960s, John Allen revolutionized the hobby with a layout that was a scale model, not a toy.
John Allen, Hayden Collection

Allen worked on his layout in Monterey, California, full time, and his modeling (along with his skill as a photographer) established new standards for realism.
John Allen, Hayden Collection

Allen's mountains stretched from floor to ceiling, dwarfing his trains. When fire destroyed his layout, magnificent scenes like this were lost forever.
John Allen, Hayden Collection

Ned Swigart's approach is that fun comes first—and for him, fun means crowding every square inch of his layout with tracks and structures.
Courtesy of the author

Swigart's Connecticut layout: a delightful cacophony of eras and scales. With no room left on the ground, he is beginning to fill the air with planes.
Courtesy of the author

Milwaukee's Jim Hediger, senior editor of MODEL RAILROADER. As modelers try to fit ever-larger layouts into small spaces, many have emulated Jim's innovative double-deck approach.
Art Schmidt for Model Railroader

Jim's Ohio Southern is a fictitious railroad,
but it is based on a real one that his parents worked for.
Jim Hediger

Bob Hayden has been building and writing about model trains since he was six. He lives in Santa Fe, where he creates museum-quality layouts for clients.
Dave Frary, Hayden Collection

The subject of Bob's first large layout that he built for himself was the Maine coast circa 1941.
Dave Frary, Hayden Collection

Bob—like John Allen—creates scenes that are products of his imagination but that look and feel exactly like real places.
Dave Frary, Hayden Collection

Tony Koester of New Jersey is
the hobby's leading advocate of
running model trains in a way
that replicates the way
real railroads operate.
Judy Koester

In his landmark layout, now dismantled,
Tony modeled the coal mining areas of West Virginia.
Tony Koester

Historical accuracy is important to Tony,
so he made frequent field trips to photograph
and measure real buildings along the main line.
Tony Koester

In operating sessions, Tony's trains are
run to a schedule determined by a printed
timetable. The smoke is dyed cotton.
Tony Koester

Here's what an operating session looks like. This large layout
was built by M.I.T. engineer John Pryke.
© *Mike Chapman*

George Sellios considered
a career in professional baseball
but wound up modeling two
huge cities for a layout that many
consider the best in the country.
Dave Frary

The cracks in the
street and the bums
crowding the sidewalk
evoke the mood of a
place that has seen
better days.
Dave Frary

George's relentless detailing transforms a minor scene like this into
a small masterpiece. His fabulous layout is in Peabody, Massachusetts.
Dave Frary

This shot is proof that George doesn't
lose his touch at the city line.
Dave Frary

John Posey and the Colorado Midland, with me, when he was six months old, and today, in our basement in Connecticut.
Photos by Ellen Griesedieck

Rolf Schneider, the wizard who built the structures and did the wiring on the Colorado Midland.
Ellen Griesedieck

Scene from my layout. Obviously, the idea was to compete with John Allen!
The Englemann Canyon Viaduct is in the background.
Tom Powel Imaging, Inc.

This western town on my
Colorado Midland is Rolf
Schneider's handiwork.
The Cielo Vista station
is on the left.
© *Christopher Little*

The yard on my layout was inspired by
the Midland's yard in Glenwood Springs.
© *Christopher Little*

The steep and twisting route of the Colorado Midland,
together with the trains' unreliable brakes, led to frequent wrecks.
Courtesy of the author

Two of the Colorado Midland's
industries: a mine (*ABOVE*) and a
Newman's Own bottling plant
(*RIGHT*). My wife, Ellen, created the
artwork for the labels on the real
Newman's Own products.
Judy Griesedieck

The Dolores River Chasm, on my layout.
The rocks are made of Styrofoam, and the river is painted Masonite.
Judy Griesedieck

The Colorado Midland was built
in the 1880s, when all locomotives
were powered by steam.
Judy Griesedieck

Wooden trestles and deep
ravines on the slopes
of Mt. Whitman.
Judy Griesedieck

Dave Frary: lobsterman,
master modeler, photographer.
He currently lives on Cape Cod.
Bob Hayden

Using subtle compositional devices, Dave draws the viewer
into the scene and makes him feel part of the action.
Dave Frary

Dave's modeling is restrained and intimate. His photography manages to convey the sense of a specific moment in time.
Dave Frary

Dave repeats the triangular shape of the foreground roof in the overall composition. Devices like this make even his most informal shots memorable.
Dave Frary

Malcolm Furlow's Ferrocarril de Rio Mantañas is the most artistically
original layout yet built, the product of a vivid imagination
and consummate modeling skills.
Malcolm Furlow

Malcolm lives in New Mexico. He is a professional artist, and he approaches his layout as if he were making a three-dimensional painting. *Malcolm Furlow*

The Ferrocarril de Rio Mantañas is rugged, funny, and exceedingly complex—a self-portrait of the man who created it. *Malcolm Furlow*

of grab handles on a boxcar and Tony being able to whip out a document that proved his case.

But the triumphs of the Nickel Plate were still a long way off. As for just how far, the man who knew best was Tony himself. After all, he had done it all before.

It was early morning and I was driving north out of Albuquerque on Interstate 25. Approaching Santa Fe, the road began a long ascent, curving gradually to the east. The rental car labored, and the sun shafted with painful intensity through a slot between the desert and a low ceiling of gray clouds. I was heading toward Bob Hayden's house, where, by prearrangement, I would join him in his SUV for the assault on Malcolm Furlow's place, an eight-hundred-acre ranch in the high scrub country two and a half hours farther north.

No sensible person goes to Malcolm Furlow's alone.

I had met Bob Hayden on a trip I made to Milwaukee shortly before *Model Railroader* published the first article on my layout. At the time, he was the editor of *Fine Scale Modeler,* another Kalmbach magazine, and *Model Railroader*'s Andy Sperandeo had taken me to his house. I was halfway down the stairs to the basement when Bob thrust a handheld controller into my hand and said, "Here, run the train. It's the best way to get to know the railroad."

The subject of the layout was Maine in 1941, just before the United States entered World War II. At first glance, I saw a harbor and a small city, while off to the left was an inland section, with a logging operation as its focal point. Bob said the room was twenty-eight feet square, but the layout seemed much larger, managing to be in front of you, beside you, and reaching away from you, all at the same time. Following the train drew me into the details: the docks, the seagulls, the fleet of fishing boats. The tide was out, and the water looked clear and cold. Inland, it was fall, the trees bright with autumn reds and yellows.

Now I was again looking at autumn colors, this time real ones, as Bob and I rolled north from Santa Fe through Tesuque and Espanola. We drove for a few miles along the Rio Chama just before it intersects the Rio Grande, and at Ojo Caliente we saw cottonwoods clustered along the bank, a sunburst of cadmium yellow mixed with gold. Then we turned onto a narrow two-lane road that led us through a landscape of junipers and pines; the pines stood apart from one another, like watchtowers. Hugging the dusty ground were the ubiquitous piñon bushes, half of them dead from a recent drought. We were at eight thousand feet and climbing.

"Out here, a hundred miles is an errand," Bob said. Bob is James Mason with a trim beard playing Captain Nemo—an apt comparison because he spent eight years in the navy, much of it aboard submarines. The eldest of five children, he grew up in the Boston area, where his father was a teacher. Bob's introduction to trains was at age six, with a Lionel setup. "It wasn't a layout," he recalls. "It was a toy that was brought out at Christmas and then put away." When he was taken to see his uncle's HO layout, he suddenly became aware of "a vast, secret world out there." ("And that was it for the Boy Scouts," a friend would later remark.) It wasn't long before his passion for this secret world led to a job in a local hobby shop.

He was just fourteen, and the job description, Bob recalls, was low man on the totem pole. "I carried shipments in from the curb, restocked the shelves, swept the floor, and when things were really slow I washed the owner's car." It was at the store that Bob met Dave Frary, and the two began a lifelong friendship. Dave was twenty and married, but the six-year age difference was dissolved by the mutuality of their interests. Bob wanted to write about model trains, and Dave wanted to photograph them. Dave was working as a firefighter, and the two spent hours together in the firehouse preparing magazine articles.

The first of the almost two hundred articles they have so far produced together was published when Bob was still in high school. The collaboration continued during Bob's years in the navy; he remembers writing articles in the wardroom of a diesel sub off Hong Kong. When his tour of duty was over, Bob landed a job at Kalmbach, where he would work for twenty-two years, until 1998. As head of their books department, he published Linn Westcott's account of John Allen's Gorre and Daphetid (Linn died with it unfinished, and Bob completed the manuscript). He also coauthored Dave's scenery book and established *Fine Scale Modeler*.

Twenty-five miles south of the Colorado border, we turned east at Tres Piedras. Bob had been to Malcolm's twice before, and after a few miles he confidently turned off the pavement onto a barely discernible desert road. Now his SUV was in its element, but Bob had his hands full steering around rocks and sagebrush. Approaching a slight rise, the road forked. We went left, and ahead I could see what looked like a small village, with the buildings ranged behind a wall. A two-story house stood off to the left along with a smaller structure topped with a stubby steeple, complete with a cross. Dead ahead, just beyond the gate, was a large, single-story building. Materials were sticks, poles, adobe, aluminum, tile, earth; the design had obviously been worked out on the spot. The clouds were hanging so low they had almost become part of the architecture.

Sharon Furlow—blond and wearing a bright red shirt— greeted us at the gate, but I was distracted by the sight of a horse and rider coming at us, fast, along the wall. The horse pulled up at the last moment, crowding us back against the gate, and a bearded man, dressed entirely in black, including a black hat, slid off the saddle to the ground, his spurs clinking as they hit the dirt.

This was Malcolm. He was shorter than he had looked a moment before on the horse, and out of breath—a different man altogether from the ominous one suggested by the charging black silhouette. The dust was still settling as he led us into the compound to show us his latest project, a large gate that reminded me of the one at the entry to the Ponderosa, the Cartwright family's ranch in the TV series *Bonanza*. Malcolm said they didn't really need a gate, at least not one that big. It was there to frame the view, which sloped off across a broad plain to the base of the Sangre de Cristo Mountains twenty miles to the southeast. Malcolm and Sharon didn't have a well (water was trucked in) and their only bathroom was a one-hole outhouse, but Malcolm had taken the time, and spent the money, to build the gate purely for aesthetic reasons.

"He never rests, never sits down," Sharon said to me, although just at that moment Malcolm *was* sitting, perched on the edge of the hearth in the living room. But his black hat was still on, along with his spurs, and he looked like a jack-in-the-box, coiled and ready to spring up at any moment.

"As soon as I have an idea, I start doing it," he said. "My first train set was brought by Santa Claus. American Flyer. I blew it up with a firecracker. Then I got some Lionel stuff, but I gave it away because I couldn't stand the third rail." He had been intrigued by the trains, however, and soon he was beginning an HO layout. He met Sharon when she was fifteen, and when they started dating they had to pick their way around the tracks to get into Malcolm's bedroom.

He raced motocross, either winning or crashing—nothing in between. He started a rock and roll band. He played the guitar and was the lead singer. The band appeared in Las Vegas, Reno, and Lake Tahoe. They had a contract with Mercury Records, and one of their songs made its way up the charts to number sixteen.

But Malcolm couldn't get model trains out of his system. "I'd come back late from a gig and then work on my layout until dawn," he recalls. When he was on the road, he built parts of trestles between engagements and stored them in his guitar case. Before long, he had given up the band and was working on trains full-time. Next, he fell in love with photography, which became inseparable from his modeling. He would position his lights and keep them on as he worked, creating a composition of light and shadow. He began constructing scenes with a picture intended as the final product, not the modeling.

His pictures were popular and easily found their way into print. In 1984, he wrote a book for Kalmbach—*HO Narrow Gauge That You Can Build*—(which inspired me to build our trestles). In 1990, he constructed an enormous layout in the lobby of a children's hospital in Houston, using closed-circuit TV to bring live pictures of the trains into the kids' rooms.

When the hospital project was finished, Malcolm thought he was through with what he called "my train thing," and he embarked on his "art thing." Like the music and the trains, this was an immediate success. He moved from Houston to Santa Fe, which along with nearby Taos was the hub of a burgeoning market for Southwestern art.

Malcolm painted in a vivid, Fauvist style, squeezing paint right from the tubes onto the canvas. He sold out show after show, pocketing as much as $5,000 apiece for pictures he could produce in a couple of days. The money piled up, and he was able to buy the ranch. He was a celebrity. He traveled to New York and Paris. He trained horses for Julia Roberts.

It wasn't enough. The old Furlow restlessness was tugging at his sleeve. But this time, he didn't want to do something new, he wanted to revert to model railroading. "A model train layout can be art," he told me flatly. "It's sculptural. It has composition. It evokes a mood—there's an emotional response."

When Malcolm had built his first layouts, his emotional responses were lighthearted. Narrow gauge locomotives puffed through the Rockies hauling swaybacked cars and passing Western towns whose inhabitants were cheerful and somewhat cartoonish. But soon a sense of foreboding had crept in. Tree trunks went from straight to twisted, skies darkened, the trestles became fragile and terrifyingly high, the towns became slums.

For one series of photographs, shot just before he gave up modeling and began painting, Malcolm had constructed a valley scene in which the rocks seemed to ooze blood, a ravine was filled with dead trees and wrecked railroad cars, and steel bridges were rusted and on the point of collapse. In the immediate foreground, clearly separated from the rest of the scene, Malcolm had placed three contemporary figures, including a Sharon-like blonde in a short, red skirt. They stood with their backs to the camera, staring into the valley as if it was a deranged world from another time.

Scenes like this, and the creative impulses that went with them, had put Malcolm in direct conflict with Tony Koester in the struggle for what model railroading should be all about. Bob Hayden had remarked, sensibly, that there was more than one hobby here and that one approach was just as legitimate as another, but as I listened to Malcolm, I wondered if I would take the chance of putting him in a room alone with Tony. Tony's total commitment to realism was equaled only by Malcolm's utter disdain for it. "Accuracy is a crutch," he said to me and went on to describe a modeler who had told him his embankments were too steep to be prototypically correct. "Can you imagine that?" he asked me, getting angry once again over an incident that had happened more than ten years ago.

Malcolm's extreme modeling was a lightning rod for people who thought the hobby should be about trains, not personal expression. He has had people call him crazy to his face. He has received hate mail. When he was living in Texas, people would come to his house and wait outside his front door for a chance to argue with him. He said, "It's as if I was violating the Holy Grail of model railroading."

When he had turned to painting, it had been a relief to leave all that animosity behind, but now that he was attempting a comeback in model railroading, he worried that the opposition had become stronger. He told me darkly that Tony and his legions of operators had gained the upper hand. "The operators will wreck it," he said, "because they don't offer people anything to look at. Scenery—that's what attracts people, gets them excited. The operators want to allude to model railroading as an art form, but when the art part actually comes up they practically run for the door."

In what Malcolm considered to be the battle for the soul of the hobby, he was losing. But he had plenty of fight left in him, and the weapon he would wield was the new layout he had just started.

The living room chat was over; it was time to visit the woodshed, which Sharon called Malcolmland.

A RAILROAD TO RUN

storm was breaking across the high country. Lightning struck the ground eighty yards beyond Malcolm's new gate, and the first drops pounded into the dust around our feet as we hurried across the courtyard to the woodshed. It was dark inside, and the rain clattered on the tin roof. Malcolm groped for the light switch.

The first thing I saw as the lights came on was a cluster of rock pinnacles. Looking like gnarly tree trunks, these "rocks" (they were made out of blue foam) extended from the floor to the underside of the woodshed's roof. The room was small, perhaps fourteen feet by twenty feet, so the high ceiling gave the space a distinctly vertical feeling, which was reinforced by the soaring rocks. Fragments of distant valleys were visible beyond the rocks, and thanks to Malcolm's clever placement of mirrors, these valleys seemed to punch through the back wall.

But where were the trains? Virtually every layout starts with a place for the tracks—a level, or nearly level, surface. The floor. A table. Shelves. No such surface existed here. Looking more closely, I saw that Malcolm had in fact stuffed some sections of track in among the pinnacles, but they didn't connect with one another, at least not yet. Tracks popped out of tunnels, crossed bridges, and disappeared into buildings—but much of the time they just ended in thin air. The curves were as tight as Lionel's, although here the distortions had the reality of a dream.

The ominous character of the last railroad scene he had built was mostly gone. His new motif (which he said Bob Hayden had brought to his attention) was a melting pot of Mexican, South American, and Cuban railroads, tequila-powered and operated by wacky, gun-toting Mexicans who were half hidden under huge sombreros. Houses and mines teetered on fragile stilts, bridges spanned other bridges, stairways led up and up ("my vertical thing," Malcolm called the effect), cactuses waved their branches like the arms of agitated kids, and anywhere you looked feverish work was taking place around machinery that seemed to be missing vital parts.

He was calling it the Ferrocarril de Rio Mantañas—the Mantañas River Railroad. The structures were all created in place. "You wouldn't make paint strokes on a palette and try to transfer them to a canvas," he said. Every surface was encrusted with grime and overlaid with many layers of paint, which fused the separate parts into a single organic mass. "I don't know how to do 'clean and shiny,' " he told us.

Malcolm envisioned the finished layout as a sculpture animated by trains. Big trains. Their scale, 1:20, was more than four times larger than HO. I picked up a locomotive and was surprised by its weight; it took both hands to hold it. "As I get older," he said, "the heft of the bigger equipment feels good." He pointed with delight to a chunky bulldozer. "You get this stuff at toy stores for next to nothing, and it all looks great." The locomotives were powered by batteries, not current from the rails, so Malcolm won't have to worry about keeping the tracks clean. "These guys just bust through all the dirt," he said.

It was intriguing to think that Tony Koester's left-brain, buttoned-down, historically unimpeachable re-creation of the Nickel Plate was being built at the same time as the Ferrocarril de Rio Mantañas. Tony wants to turn model railroading into a game with rules. Malcolm, by contrast, thinks of it as a highly personal means of expression, with no rules.

Like the differences between the fort guys and the train guys, this is a line drawn in the sand.

John Pryke is on Tony's side.

John Pryke (rhymes with *bike*) has a layout inspired by a single day in the life of the New Haven Railroad: September 3, 1948, when eight-year-old John watched a New Haven express train blast through Old Saybrook, Connecticut, at 65 mph. His railroad (like Jim's and Tony's) was designed for operation, which is to say that certain carefully chosen individuals are invited on a regular basis to help him run it. One night, I came to watch.

John lives half an hour west of Boston. Following his directions, I made turn after turn, as if in a labyrinth, until I came to a dead-end street. John's gray gambrel was up the slope to my right, half buried in a forest of mature oaks and maples. The operators, eight of them, arrived within a few moments of one another and went directly down to the basement. They brought the doughnuts; John's wife, Sandy, made coffee. We gathered around a workbench, which was set against a wall covered with framed certificates of the host's model contest victories, along with his four *Model Railroader* covers.

In a few days, the layout was to be filmed by a commercial video maker, which would give John the grand slam of model railroading: the covers, a book, the appearance in Kalmbach's annual *Great Model Railroads,* and the video. At sixty-three, he is a member of the hobby's old guard (he knew John Allen), and he is enjoying a renaissance at *Model Railroader,* where he is currently billed as their guru of weathering.

John suffers from polycythemia, an excess of red corpuscles; he has to have his blood pumped out once a month. When I visited, he had hurt his back moving an air conditioner, so his movements were cautious. He wore jeans and a checked shirt, but his manner was coat-and-tie. "I was driven by a strict upbringing," he told me during the chat we had before the session began. His father, a mechanical engineer, was English. "He expected one hundred percent, not ninety-nine percent," John said, "and one of the reasons I got into model railroading was that it set the stage for overachieving."

When he was twenty, he began work on a scratch-built locomotive. The project took 1,500 hours and won him first prize at a national convention. "I was just a kid," he recalled, "and here's Linn Westcott introducing himself, eager to run a spread on my locomotive."

Following his father into mechanical engineering, John enrolled at MIT. His thesis was a design for a variable gauge system that actually got built in Africa, but John never made any money off the invention because he didn't have the $500 filing fee for the patent. "At MIT there were geniuses and grunts," he said, "and I was a grunt." Some grunt. He did heat balance programs for nuclear reactors and worked on an "electric brain," a transistor-ized computer that took up three rooms.

The moment for coffee and doughnuts was brief, and now the operators were positioned around the layout, visible from the shoulders up, looming like Easter Islanders in the scenery. Most worked at the high-tech jobs that are typical of the area. One was a semiconductor design engineer, another a designer of fault management systems for computers. The group also included an architect and an electrical engineer. Each had donned a headset, so John's briefing was delivered in a conversational tone.

Then the trains began to move, with the operators following the printed timetable like a script. The trains were assigned spe-cific routes, and each quickly assumed its own character within the choreography of the whole. Here was a streamliner (the *Yan-kee Clipper,* or the *Merchant's Limited*) running wide-open along the main line, stopping only at the terminal stations such as Prov-idence or New London. Here was the "fish train," a fast, fifteen-car freight favored with special rights of way thanks to its perishable cargo. Other, slower freights meandered along from town to town, always ceding the main line to the more important trains. A husband-and-wife team shunted cars in one yard, seventy-seven-year-old Ellis Walker worked another, while ac-tivities in a port city (the subject of John's book, *Building City Scenery*) were directed by Vic Hamburger, whose name was let-tered on trucks and a warehouse: V. HAMBURGER & CO., FINE POULTRY AND MEATS. Switches buzzed. The operators spoke quietly into their headsets. It was September 3, 1948.

Tony Koester had written of a layout "coming alive" during an operating session, and now I saw that because the trains—up to seven at a time, not counting the switch engines—were inter-acting with one another instead of merely doing laps, watching them was like following a story. Or, in this case, a collection of stories, because every five minutes or so a particular sequence of maneuvers would be completed, and the trains would all be brought to a stop.

The session lasted two hours, and in the end John was satisfied that the layout was in working order for the video. John Allen had followed his operating sessions with a second round of coffee and conversation that could last until after midnight. Not John Pryke. Within five minutes, the operators were on their way out the door. As I walked down the path to my car, the lights of the house were turned out behind me.

John takes his model railroading seriously because he is a serious man. Engineers, after all, tend to be that way. However, he can laugh at himself. Hanging along with his framed covers and awards is a cartoon depicting a provocative nude standing next to a layout while the modeler, angered by the distraction, says, "For God's sake, Gilda, I've got a railroad to run."

When Dave Frary was little, his family lived next to the tracks, and the story goes that he would stand up in his playpen to watch the trains. His first layout, the familiar Lionel four-by-eight-foot, became the subject for his early efforts at photography. He set up his scenes on the kitchen table. Soon, he switched to HO for more realism. With money from his paper route, he bought a small HO locomotive. Next, he acquired three freight car kits, mailing in cereal box tops along with $2.

Meanwhile, he frequented the library, signing out, over time, almost one hundred books on photography and reading them all. "I'd see a picture," he said, "and wonder how it was shot. I'd go to great lengths to figure it out." He was an art major at the University of Massachusetts, and afterward he worked for NASA as a photographer, having used his model railroad pictures to help get the job. He also served a boring stretch as the audiovisual director for the local school system. "I hated it," he told me.

What Dave needed was a way to make a living out of his modeling and photography. He had built a superb layout, which the magazines featured regularly. But it was his book, *How to Build Realistic Model Railroad Scenery,* that really put Dave on the map. Written in collaboration with Bob Hayden and published in 1982 by Kalmbach's book division (which Bob was running), it has sold, to date, more than 350,000 copies in thirty-seven editions. The book was significant in the hobby because Dave was the first serious modeler to use latex paint exclusively, and he based his intricate formulas on water-soluble acrylics and polymers. Before Dave, modelers used slow-drying plasters, oil paint, shellac, and vinegar; the smell of turpentine was a train room signature. Overnight, *How to Build Realistic Model Railroad Scenery* made all that stuff obsolete.

In addition to his model railroad activities, Dave was a full-time lobster fisherman, based out of Swampscott, Massachusetts. He was on the water from six in the morning until noon; after that, unloading and cleaning up took until four, a long day that he would follow with a full evening of work on his trains. At his peak, Dave fished eight hundred pots; today, he is virtually retired from lobstering and has just one hundred.

His latest model railroading enterprise is once again a partnership with Bob. They build custom layouts, typically for rich enthusiasts who want a trophy layout but haven't the time, or the skill, to do it themselves. (This is the outer edge of the trend Walthers has been exploiting with its preassembled buildings.) Most of their jobs have been out west. Adjacent to Bob's house in Santa Fe is a building that is a small factory for the construction of model train layouts. It has an office, a workshop, and a large area for building the layouts, which are disassembled, shipped, and then finished off at the client's house.

Bob and Dave will also work entirely on site. Dave flies in from Massachusetts, while Bob drives, his car loaded with supplies. Then the two men go to work, typically ten hours a day, for eight-day stretches. These are not minor league layouts. A recent project for a Tucson man measured twenty-five by fifty feet. An artist was employed, full-time, just to paint the backdrop. Bob and Dave are fast. Dave said, "We work just like an old married couple—never a wasted move." They're not cheap; a layout can require up to eight sessions, at $10,000 apiece.

"We show up," Dave continued, "and maybe the client doesn't have a vision of what he wants. But he'll have some pictures. The exciting part is when we wind up building exactly what he wanted, only he didn't know he wanted it. You start, you finish. It's great because it isn't in *your* basement, and you don't have to worry about what to do next. You shoot some photographs, and you move on." That is, you get the fun of building layouts, and you make a living at the same time.

Outside the world of HO, custom-built layouts have had a long tradition. Lionel's, at their showroom in New York, served as the prototype. Jammed with tracks, trains, and accessories, it was basically a great big toy, the setup under the Christmas tree taken to an extreme. But custom-built HO layouts are relatively new. Traditionally, HO only attracted people who wanted to do things for themselves and who wished to express their creativity through their layout's design and scenery. Pride of authorship. Self-reliance. Today, however, you can forget all that. Just dial up Dave and Bob.

The current cost of *How to Build Realistic Model Railroad Scenery* is $18.95. A custom layout will run you tens of thousands.

Is there something in between? There is. And Dave and Bob are involved in that, too.

It is 9 P.M. in a conference room in the Hawthorne Hotel in Salem, Massachusetts, and five men are clustered around Bob, who is demonstrating airbrush technique. *Phhsssst. Phhssssssst.* He is weathering a boxcar. Anyone who has ever used an airbrush knows they clog up. Always. But Bob's never does. He will tell you why, at the Model Railroad Skills Institute, a sort of Outward Bound for modelers. The Institute was dreamed up by a video producer named Allen Keller and given the blessing of *Model Railroader.* Cost for the four-day session: $1,700.

You could also watch Dave Frary make mountains and listen to Tony Koester lecture on layout design and operation. Additional speakers are newspaper editor Henry Freeman, who could tell you how to research historical information, and Allen Keller himself, who is about to film John Pryke's layout. Each member of this so-called faculty wears his Model Railroad Skills Institute shirt, complete with the Institute's semaphore logo. A twenty-foot-long layout, nicknamed the Plywood Pacific, had been assembled for demonstrations. Many trains are on hand, including the new, unobtainable Broadway Limited steamer with its revolutionary sound package. Enlarged photographs of the Gorre and Daphetid are propped up against the walls. A field trip is planned to view a layout built by master modeler George Sellios.

Talent. Props. Enthusiasm. But only seven students. Two have taken the course before, which leaves only five new faces, and one of these, a set designer from Spokane, has won the trip in a contest and is here for free. The seminars began five years before and have never really caught on; it is possible this one will be the last. Dinner conversation echoes the lament of the aging

Catskill resort owner in the movie *Dirty Dancing,* who wonders why the young people no longer come.

One theory is that $1,700 is too much. But the two repeaters, one of whom is a jet pilot, insists it is a bargain. Perhaps, then, the four days, plus travel, is too long. But no; modelers spend thousands of hours on their layouts. When Skip Barber started what would become an immensely successful school for racing drivers, he set out to prove that fast driving, until then mythologized as purely instinctive, was actually a teachable skill. In model railroading, it is a question of whether people *want* to be taught. Here is a highly individual hobby, and most of the people engaged in it work alone. To them, the appeal is that you teach yourself. During the airbrush demonstration, Bob says, deadpan, "At some point you might have to break down and read the instructions," but no one laughs.

Perhaps the expert's knowledge, often so hard-won, just doesn't matter that much to the average modeler. It is great to hear about the track-cleaning virtues of Wahl Oil, which professional barbers use to lubricate hair clippers, but other products do the job, too, and it might be fun to discover one for yourself. Dave Frary could take you step-by-step through his foolproof techniques for making rock cliffs, but guys like me are happy to blunder along on their own. Tony Koester distributes a kit for planning an "operating" layout, but not everyone wants a track plan with the rigor of a chess game.

The Institute offers a middle ground between full-service custom modeling and the good old do-it-yourself approach, but instead of creating a profitable niche market, it has managed to fall between the cracks.

Too bad, I thought later, after Bob's airbrushing session. But my mind was already on the next day, when I was going to see a layout I had every reason to think was the best in the country.

I parked at a meter in downtown Peabody, crossed the street, and walked past a combination deli and jewelry store, a karate parlor, and a secondhand clothes store until I came to an unmarked door, which had been squeezed between the stores like an afterthought. Beyond the door was a steep flight of stairs. Waiting for me in the dim light at the top was George Sellios.

He has been described as a recluse, but he welcomed me warmly and seemed pleased to have a visitor. He was slim and moved like an athlete as he led me along a narrow corridor to the front of the building. We sat down in chairs by a window with a view of the street. He was in his late fifties, but his trim mustache, white shirt, and black chinos gave him the look of a much younger man.

His first trains had been Lionel, but in order to rid himself of their third rail he soon exchanged them for American Flyer. He built a four-by-eight-foot layout that had legs at the corners but no other supports, so it sagged in the middle. When he was eleven, he bought an issue of *Railroad Model Craftsman* that featured a model of a grain mill built by a man named Lloyd Giebner. At first, George thought the photograph was a shot of the real thing. Something clicked when he realized it was a *model;* he was staggered by the idea that such realism was possible. He had been making structures out of cigar boxes, painting windows and doors right on the wood. Now he tried to build Giebner's mill. Disappointed with his first attempt, he tried again. By his fourth try, he was close—and hooked on the excitement of seeing something that looked so real take shape in his hands.

He was also hooked on baseball, which he played throughout his teenage years. His goal was to be the center fielder for a major league team, and he was good enough to be invited for a tryout by the Minnesota Twins. He reported to training camp—only to discover he couldn't cope with the speed of major league pitching. "Just looking at one eighty-five-mile-per-hour fastball was enough to convince me I didn't have a future in the pros," he told me.

He came home to Peabody and began to design and manufacture scale model kits, some of which had more than one thousand parts. Overnight, these kits became the industry standard. Producing them was George's livelihood, and ironically it wasn't until 1985, when he was forty, that he was able to make time to begin his own layout. He called it the Franklin and South Manchester.

"I am an artist," he told me. Like many artists, he was inspired by a precursor, whose work he used as a point of departure for his own. That master was, as with so many modelers, John Allen. But instead of Allen's signature landscapes, George was attracted to a city Allen had included in his layout. Called Port, it had a foreground of chilly seawater, beaten-up tugs and scows, pilings, and docks. Office buildings, several of which were fifteen stories tall, crowded the waterfront. The trains crept through on tracks laid right on the wharfs.

George wasn't the first to copy Port, but he did what few have been able to do: he beat Allen at his own game. George took his sizable loft and filled it with two model cities, which he called Manchester and Dovertown. From one end to the other measured more than forty feet. Beyond the cities, stretching for many scale miles, he built a rural landscape that is currently about 90 percent complete.

The Institute group arrived. After some commotion as introductions were made, I was aware of a sudden hush as everyone began to stare at the layout. Over the years, thousands of people have visited the Franklin and South Manchester (it is open to the public once a month, on Saturday mornings), and George is used to that silence. It may be why he doesn't hesitate to call himself an artist.

The layout is built on a waist-high platform, and the taller buildings disappear into the ceiling, which is about twelve feet above the floor. It is lit by dozens of bright museum-quality lights and framed by a black valance above and a black skirt board below. The enormous weight of the city seems to float in space.

The detailing is overwhelming. You discover more going on in every square foot, every square *inch,* than seems possible . . . and then you realize it isn't just this one part that George has handled this way, it's the *whole thing.* He has modeled every sort of material: brick, concrete, glass, copper, tar paper, tin, wood, steel. Every surface has been textured, painted, smudged, scraped, scoured, stained, and weathered.

Soon the group's awed silence gave way to an excited buzz of conversation. The old hands, such as Dave Frary, who had photographed the layout, and Allen Keller, who had shot videos here, acted as enthusiastic as those of us who were first-timers. Even Tony Koester, who knew George had little interest in operation, could be heard mumbling about what a great layout it was.

The period is the mid-1930s, during the Depression. George used more than two thousand figures, each one hand-painted and playing a role in a carefully crafted vignette. A man sits hunched on a toilet in an alley, under an Ex-Lax sign, while another pisses against a wall. Hobos are gathered around a fire (the flames actually appear to flicker) playing poker with miniature cards so detailed you can make out the hand each man has drawn. Sidewalks are cracked and sprouting weeds. Dogs sniff at garbage cans. Pipes leak. Gutters sag. Sewage pours into the harbor. A policeman has just tucked a parking ticket under a windshield wiper. A bullet-riddled car (Al Capone's?) is being towed away.

A twenty-story building with perhaps five hundred windows, each detailed slightly differently, stands next to a building with six hundred windows, next to one with four hundred fifty, and so on. Peering over and around the buildings, I caught glimpses of hidden courtyards detailed every bit as elaborately as the scenery that is out in full view. I asked George how he decided that enough was enough, and he said there could never be too much. He said he takes great pains to detail things you would never expect (like having the rear window of a car rolled down so that you can see a pile of junk in the backseat).

John Allen's city had been a bustling place where the offices were full and the stevedores and construction workers had plenty to do. George's is a decaying inner city where the life has gone from the tall buildings, whose windows stare vacantly across at other empty windows. Walls and fire escapes are overgrown with ivy. A warehouse has burned (George built a model and, literally, put a match to it), and its charred remains have been left abandoned. Signs and billboards give the layout a voice as you read them to yourself: *Lagenbeck-Wallace, Connecticut Seed Tobacco, Moxie, Willard Batteries, Sisson's Diner, Borax.*

Life is in the streets, where bums live on black coffee and straight whiskey. In the harbor, the murky green water is slick with oil. This was the world of the artists of the Ash Can School, like George Bellows, whose 1913 cityscape *The Cliff Dwellers* has colors that match the layout's: umbers, deep maroons, ochers, slate grays, and charcoal blacks, all dulled with the patina of age.

It is the presence of the trains, however, around which scene after scene revolves. A freight train moves slowly down a crowded city street. Boxcars are parked on a siding at the base of a five-story warehouse. A commuter train glides through a yard, suggesting that suburbs lie beyond the city. The locomotives are all steamers, streaked with soot. The rolling stock, passenger cars included, are so heavily weathered as to be camouflaged amid the crumbling walls and rusting metal fences beside the main line. The dark trains slither like eels along the bottom of the urban canyons. Tracks vanish into tunnels, under buildings, and down narrow streets, leading trains into an unseen world that is full of foreboding.

Just as individual brushstrokes show an artist's touch, the Franklin and South Manchester is plainly the work of a man with boundless energy. "I work fast," George said, echoing Dave Frary. He told me he could assemble, and weather, one of his twenty-story buildings in just two or three days. He built the whole layout working eight to five, three months a year, for seventeen years, which is about a third of the time it took John Allen to build the Gorre and Daphetid.

Inspired by a master, George Sellios has built a masterpiece.

B O R R O W E D T I M E

When my daughter, Judy, was thir-teen, she and a friend built a layout for me for Christmas. My excite-ment grew as word filtered up from the basement that work was going well. Since I had been hard-pressed to find any women involved with the hobby, I sensed a cultural break-through was at hand. *And it was happening right here, in our basement!*

On the big day, I was escorted downstairs. The layout was stunning. The girls had carved blue foam for the landforms, then added Gerry Bill's old structures along with some of my unused scenery material. They had created a large town with a busy main street leading to a beach. Other features included a helipad, two natural-gas stor-age tanks, and a ridge with trees and houses.

In fact, all that was missing were the tracks.

The following summer, a friend arrived at our house with her nine-year-old son Thomas. Thomas was on vacation. Could he look at the trains? Sure. An hour passed, and I thought perhaps I should see how Thomas was doing. Turns out he was doing just fine. He had found a few of our leftover sections of Flextrak and installed them, neatly, around the edge of Judy's town.

Trains are a guy thing.

Judy doesn't dislike trains, nor, I suspect, do most women. *Model Railroader* often depicts wives involved in their husbands' model railroading, typically helping with the painting or building and decorating structures. My mother, of course, wired my original layout—and she enjoyed running it, too. But layouts built entirely by women are rare. Gerri Doebelin, a former surgical scrub nurse from Columbus, Ohio, created the handsome Unprototype and Scenyked Harbor Railroad, but finding others like her is a tough assignment. Joshua Cowen included Sister in his promotional shots, but she was invariably in the background. And, for the most part, that is where she has remained.

Building and operating model trains is an essentially gratuitous endeavor, trains for the sake of trains. By and large, it is a solitary activity and nothing comes of it, no product or service, that could be described as useful to society in any conventional sense. But men connect with model trains anyway, perhaps because it is part of our heritage (real trains, after all, were run by men), perhaps because it is in our nature to seek control in life through the mastery of machines—even if, in the case of model railroading, that machine is only a miniature version, a kind of symbol, of the real thing, which once meant so much.

Not only are trains for men, it seems that among modelers at the top level they may be only for men who are the oldest (or only) sons in their family. Incredibly, Tony Koester, Jim Hediger,

John Pryke, Malcolm Furlow, Bob Hayden, Dave Frary, and George Sellios were all oldest boys—that is, seven out of seven of the big-time modelers I visited. (And you can add John Allen and Rolf Schneider to the list.) This is because if the dad likes trains himself, he bought them at the first appropriate moment for, naturally, his oldest son. Then father and son bonded over the trains, just as in the Lionel ads. Boys coming along later didn't have the same chance. Walthers vice president John Sanheim's theory that grown men return to their childhood enthusiasms is just part of the story: trains also recall Dad, his love, and the sense of privilege that went with being the recipient of such a singular gift.

The other startling commonality among the top modelers I met is that they have beards! Forget my friend's thought that the world of model railroading is populated by geeks or nerds—it's a world of the *hirsute*. John, Malcolm, Bob, and Dave have beards, while George has a mustache. Only Tony and Jim are clean-shaven.

The connection between beards and trains is obvious. Consider the front of a steam locomotive. It is strikingly anthropomorphic. When I saw John's first steam engine smiling at me from the glass case at Berkshire Hills, I wasn't inventing that smile. Thanks to slight changes in the arrangements of components such as the headlight, the smokestack, and the cylinders, steam locomotives can look aloof, cross-eyed, surprised, perplexed, benign, or even angry. Virtually all steam locomotives have narrow steel ladders, one on each side, that begin at the sides of the big round smokebox (the locomotive's "face") and extend down to the top of the cowcatcher. This combination of ladders and cowcatcher unquestionably resembles a beard.

What a bearded modeler sees when he looks in the mirror each morning is nothing less than a locomotive.

=====

Jim Hediger said he liked the way modelers start with the same basic elements but wind up with different results. The diversity within the hobby is amazing. One man built a round layout geared to rotate at the speed of the train, so you could sit in one place and watch the scenery, not the train, go by. The artist Chris Burden built a giant sphere with tracks poking in and out of it. A diner in New York used a train, chugging along the counter, to deliver food to its patrons. Layouts have been installed in coffee tables and drawers and briefcases.

The Lionel layout designed by musician Neil Young was as brilliantly creative as Young himself—and it was built with a unique control system so that it could be operated by his son, who has cerebral palsy. Ward Kimball was an Oscar-winning animator for Walt Disney (he drew Jiminy Cricket), but his great passion was trains, and he inspired his boss to make them a prominent part of the Disneyland experience. Frank Sinatra's layout was housed in a full-sized reproduction of a Lionel freight station that he had constructed on the grounds of his Palm Springs estate.

But no matter what form your layout took, you were, deep down, either an operator or a scenery man. Consider the differences between the operators, like John, Tony, and Jim, and the scenery makers, like Malcolm, George, and Dave. The technical men tended toward operation, while those with liberal arts backgrounds were drawn to scenery—in other words, the way they thought about trains was connected with impulses powerful enough to have guided their choices of profession.

It was also possible to see a connection between the technical men and the need for control. Of course, anyone who builds a layout is creating a world that he can control. But the degree varies from art major Dave Frary ("I'm happy just to pour a drink and watch a train do laps through the scenery") to operators like MIT man John Pryke, who seek dominion over timetables, a half dozen trains, and ten grown-ups. The operators also tend to see trains as vehicles on a literal journey that has a beginning, middle, and end. People who are content to watch trains do laps see them more abstractly, as objects in motion, or even objects that, in their lapping, suggest the cycles of life.

In a *Model Railroader* editorial in September 1970, Linn Westcott boasted that the average age of people in the hobby was thirty-three. (Boasted, because it was thought at the time to be just for kids, and Linn wanted his readers to understand that grown-ups were interested in model trains, too.) In the late 1980s, however, Linn's point had become rather too obvious: the modelers' average age had climbed to forty-three. Today, Walthers's John Sanheim told me it is fifty-five. In my travels many of the hobbyists I talked to feared model railroading was living on borrowed time.

On a recent trip to New York, I returned to the Red Caboose for the first time since my harried visit before Christmas years ago, when I had hoped to buy a great locomotive for John. The Caboose was in the same block, but it had moved across the street, and instead of taking an elevator up, you walked down a flight, into a basement.

When I arrived, the man behind the desk was on the phone, arguing so loudly I thought at first that the store must be full of customers. However, I was the only one. A cat was asleep on a stack of boxes containing Athearn locomotives; the shelves were dusty and swaybacked with merchandise that appeared to have gone untouched since the store relocated. I hung around for ten minutes, hoping to ask a few questions about the state of the hobby, but when the man finished his call he vanished into a back room, slamming the door. I decided that to buy something in this store would require both imagination and fortitude. I was happy to escape back up to the street, and I told myself things would be better at my next stop.

FAO Schwarz, too, had moved, but it was still palatial. Visiting Schwarz as a kid, I had always bypassed the first floor and its display of enormous stuffed animals, heading instead for the stairs, which swept up in a handsome right-hand arc. At the top, no deferred gratification for me: I went straight to the Lionel layout, near the sunny windows. It was smaller than the one in Lionel's own showroom downtown on Twenty-sixth Street, but it wasn't so cluttered.

Now as I entered the store I noticed that the stuffed animals were still there, some of them bigger than ever—as if, going unsold all these years, they had continued to grow. I asked for the trains and was directed to an escalator. The new upper floor wasn't open and airy like the old one; it was choked with aisles and resembled a warehouse. Again I asked for the trains, receiving from a cheerful blond girl a beaming, polite response that made me feel quite special to be someone who was on his way to something as central to the store's identity as the train display.

Canyons of games. Action figures. Lego World. Plastic Hummers. Apparently, the management was using the appeal of the trains to generate traffic past these lesser toys. I had to be close.

Actually, I was there. The train layout was a piece of furniture, sort of. At least it was being used that way by a weary Japanese family who were sitting on it. Here in this most obscure corner of the store (I finally understood this), they had found a quiet refuge and had removed their shoes. The "layout" was a Plexiglas box about eighteen inches high and partly covered in wood. Through the family's legs, I glimpsed a large locomotive silently doing laps on a circular track. Maybe I had seen too many animals downstairs, but I was reminded of a lion or tiger at the zoo, pacing in its cage.

Depressing. Did railroading no longer appeal to kids the way it had when I was growing up? A love of trains came easily in the days when steam engines and crack transcontinental limiteds stirred the imagination. But what about today? Those exciting trains are gone—does that mean that when the last generation to have experienced them firsthand dies off, the hobby will die with them?

Bob Hayden doesn't think so, and he makes his point based on something he observed during his years as editor of *Fine Scale Modeler.* "The most popular and collectible military figures," Bob told me, "weren't the contemporary soldiers, they were the soldiers of the Napoleonic wars. There was no firsthand connection—the collectors only knew about them through books. But they went for that era anyway, because of its timeless glamor."

Kids who came along right after railroading's golden age compared the glory of the recent past with what they saw in front of them, which was a decaying system apparently headed for oblivion. So it was no surprise that they turned to other things. But now enough time has gone by for Bob's scenario to play out, for people to see railroading the way his readers appreciated Napoleonic soldiers.

Kids, especially, have few preconceptions; they like a toy on its own merits. Consider the success of Thomas the Tank Engine. After FAO Schwarz, I went to a Toys Я Us and discovered a large display area brimming with Thomas books, videos, mugs, T-shirts, and various sizes of toy trains, including HO. Thomas was created, in England, half a century ago by an Anglican clergyman named Wilbert Awdry. His son had scarlet fever, and to help him pass the time during his convalescence, Awdry invented a series of stories about a group of friendly locomotives who shared the same roundhouse.

Thomas is based on a lowly switch engine, and the term *tank* indicates that the little locomotive's water supply is carried in a reservoir surrounding the boiler rather than in a tender pulled behind. The fact that Thomas is based on a European prototype, and the stories take place on the imaginary island of Sodor, does not appear to bother American kids at all.

Thomas and his other engine friends such as Percy and James have expressive faces painted right on their smokeboxes. They are always steaming out of their roundhouse to encounter adventure. In one video, James is stung by bees. In another, naughty passenger cars called Annie and Claribell escape down the tracks. Chases and wrecks are frequent. The railroad's boss man, Sir Topham Hatt, rewards good behavior and punishes bad, but he is stuffy and it's fun when an engine gets away with something.

Thomas is big business. A feature film in which he starred has grossed more than $50 million, and the company that controls the media rights was recently sold for almost $200 million.

The appeal of Thomas and his friends gets kids interested in trains at an early age. But as those kids grow older, what is the next step?

Electronics.

In recent years, electronics have brought new life to model railroading. Digital Command Control (DCC) has eliminated the need for the complex wiring that defeated me (and I wasn't alone). All the isolated blocks, soldering, and toggles that were a necessary part of reversing polarity—gone. With DCC you control your locomotive with a handheld throttle, adjusting its speed, turning the headlight on and off, and causing the new on-board sound systems (also electronic) to produce the effects you choose. DCC makes it possible to run several trains independently over the same stretch of track, which simulates the way real railroads operate. DCC can be used by anyone, but an increasing number of hobbyists actually know what is going on in those black boxes. The magazines are filled with terms such as "logic circuit," "auto-synchronization," and "anti-chatter"; the brave new world has come to model railroading.

In other areas, however, electronic products seem to have grown out of what computers can do (and the desire to grab a share of the market), rather than any compelling need for them, and so far they appear to have appealed to people on the margins of the hobby rather than to those at its core. Nonetheless, some of these products are fascinating and may someday catch on, perhaps in an altered form.

For example, the Computer Assisted Design (CAD) software that is so familiar to engineers, designers, and architects has been adapted to allow you to draw track plans and model terrain in 3D. You can even run trains. You refine your design electronically—no mess, no wasted plywood, no piles of blue foam—and once you have the layout the way you want it, the program obligingly prints full-scale plans and templates. It is also possible to develop a layout, store it in the computer's memory, then create another. And another. (Modelers who collect unbuilt kits can now collect unbuilt layouts.)

With the advent of Microsoft's Train Simulator (MSTS) and Auran's Trainz, you can create tracks, locomotives, rolling stock, smoke, sound, buildings, and landscape—a virtual railroad. Hundreds of miles of existing prototype main lines have already been modeled, and you can watch them roll by from the cab (where you control the speed), or from the caboose. You are not restricted to railroads that are offered commercially; you might wish to design your own virtual layout. If you are Tony Koester, you can obsess over every virtual rivet. Or you could become a layout archaeologist and, as one group is considering doing, produce an electronic re-creation of John Allen's Gorre and Daphetid. Electronic modelers are even known by a name: train simmers.

But the future is uncertain for the train simmers. As Bob Hayden points out, it takes a long time to master a CAD software program, and few hobbyists feel it's worth the effort if they are going to build just one layout, which is all most of us will ever do. *Model Railroader*'s editor, Terry Thompson, sees potential in this virtual world, but he hopes that it will function not so much as an end in itself but as a way of drawing people into the hobby and getting them to the point where they will, in time, want to get their hands on some *models*.

As for me, although I liked the idea of simulation, I wasn't about to trade my basement layout for anything on a screen. And if model trains were better than virtual ones, how about the real thing?

I was planning a trip to Florida, and I thought, Why not take the train?

THE SILVER METEOR

It had been a long time since I had ridden a train for more than a short distance, but the memories of my own golden age of train travel were still fresh. In 1951, when I was seven, I was already a veteran of several trips from New York to Florida (and back). This meant that I was an old hand at going to the Pennsylvania Station, and it may be that my experience in this building was the beginning of my love not only for trains, but for architecture, too.

The station had been opened in 1910, and it covered two city blocks—almost eight acres. Cars could be driven right inside through a narrow gap between huge classical columns at the left end of the long facade. A cobblestone ramp led down to the drop-off area, which was a madhouse of slamming doors, police whistles, and porters wrestling with baggage. But it was suddenly quiet as you entered the General Waiting Room, a vast hall that I would later learn had been modeled on the Baths of Caracalla. Here, the air felt denser than the air outside. The light came from arched windows at least ten stories up, slanting down to create shining pools on the polished floor. Thomas Wolfe wrote that the Waiting Room was "murmurous with the immense and distant sounds of time."

Adjacent to the Waiting Room was the Concourse, also vast. But instead of travertine marble, the material here was steel, painted black. The columns stood out in the open, where you could see what they held up: a roof of steel lattice and glass, an umbrella of ribs and arches that looked as if someone had just finished bolting it all together. I have read that the station's architect, Charles Follen McKim, of McKim, Meade, and White, thought that after the traveler had experienced the grand classicism of the Waiting Room, he needed to go through an intermediate step before he was confronted with the high-tech trains lurking below. I'm not sure that my sensibilities were so delicate as to require this transitional space, but I loved the Concourse, which resembled an Erector set and had diffused gray light seeping through the glass canopy, seeming to come from everywhere and nowhere.

The trains were below the Concourse, reached by stairs that stretched straight down for three stories. As you descended, the light faded quickly to a gelid gloom, and the trains themselves seemed to provide the illumination. First you saw their rounded roofs, then their sleek silver sides, which were streaked with the grime of winter. The platform blocked a view of the wheels, so the cars seemed to float, shimmering, on steam that drifted up from an invisible source below. They looked, I thought, like Lionel's silver passenger cars my mother had given me for my layout.

On these trips, our family's destination in Florida was an island off the west coast called Boca Grande. In those days Boca Grande could be reached only by train or boat, the train being for a few exhilarating minutes virtually at sea as it crept across a trestle more than a mile long. The island was the end of the line. Beyond its southern tip lay nothing but water, and the porter carried a fishing rod that he used while the train was being turned around and readied for its return trip.

We went on the *Silver Meteor,* which was operated by the Seaboard Air Line (the company was founded in 1900, and "air line" referred to the directness of its routes, not to planes). Typically, we had two compartments, joined by a narrow door. My mother and grandmother would be in one, and I would be in the other. Each room had two wide seats, with a table between them that jutted out below the window. At night, the table could be removed and the seats converted into a berth; a second berth swung down from the ceiling. The surfaces were hard, but I always felt cozy and safe on the train. My compartment was a refuge, the window like the mouth of a cave, a place to view the passing world—a world that on my last trips south I could see was changing in a hurry.

By 1958, when I was fourteen, my train-riding days were essentially over. The interstate highways were being built and the Boeing 707 jet was making travel by plane popular for many, including our family. The railroads went into rapid decline, their freight business lost to trucks and their passenger business to cars and planes.

Once we stopped taking the train to Florida, I never went back to Penn Station. But I followed the story of its demise. When the Pennsylvania Railroad started to go broke, their beleaguered executives began cutting costs wherever they could. They stopped maintaining the station, which deteriorated in a hurry. Then the Pennsy's management lifted their ban on advertising, and overnight a motley collection of hastily installed signs and vending machines filled the station. In an awkward attempt at modernization, the ticket counter was rebuilt along the west side of the Waiting Room, where it blocked circulation. Automobiles revolving on turntables and the new ticket counter's roof, which was fluorescent and shaped like an airfoil, reminded passengers of both the cars and the planes that were bringing the Pennsy to its knees.

The next step was to call in the real estate developers, who convinced the railroad's management that the station's high ceilings were nothing but wasted space. A plan emerged to tear the station down and erect an office building and an all-new Madison Square Garden sports center in its place. (The station would still be there, relocated in what amounted to the basement.) Demolition began shortly after the plan's approval, and before preservationists could get organized.

I remember seeing photographs of giant cranes inside the Waiting Room, which reminded me just how big the dying station really was. Shots of dump trucks hauling away the remains of Corinthian columns made me vaguely uneasy, yet, as a nineteen-year-old looking to the future, I failed to grasp that New York was losing something irreplaceable.

Forty years after the destruction of the station, I was once again planning to go to Boca Grande. I was delighted to find that the *Silver Meteor* was still running, now as an Amtrak-operated train. Amtrak didn't offer connections to the island, but I could ride as far as Orlando, then finish the trip in a rental car. I bought a ticket, one way. Point-to-point. I knew the *Silver Meteor* would revive some memories and take me back to the earliest days of my love for trains, when my Lionel layout was teaching me remote control and the real trains I rode on were showing me the great wide world that I hoped someday to explore.

We were scheduled to depart at 7 P.M. In spite of Amtrak's ongoing financial difficulties, trains in general were making a modest comeback. No single event had reversed the decline, but railroads had proven to be stubborn in the face of extinction, slowly reinventing themselves in ways that were enabling them to survive and in some cases even prosper. The high-speed Acela, operating between Boston and Washington, was a success. Grand Central Terminal had been beautifully restored and was reporting average daily passenger counts of 240,000, exceeding even the busiest days during World War II. As for Penn Station itself, it had recently undergone a $200-million-dollar rehabilitation by the Long Island Rail Road, which improved the connections between the LIRR's commuter trains and the city's subway system.

It was snowing as I approached the station, which made this seem like a particularly good time to be traveling to Florida. I was caught up in a crowd surging toward the doors. Fellow passengers! Filled with bonhomie, I asked a woman next to me where she was going. Going? She gave me an odd look. That's when I discovered that everyone except me was headed upstairs to a concert in Madison Square Garden. Next, I realized the LIRR's renovations were to another part of the building. Where I was, at Amtrak's concourse, reminded me of a food court at a suburban mall. The perimeter was formed by adjoining restaurants, their names, in neon, strung so close together they could be seen as reading in combinations: *Nathan'sRoy-Rogers, Houlihan'sPizzaHut*. The ceiling was disproportionally low, as if the designers had vengefully repudiated the glory of the original.

The Amtrak waiting room resembled the lobby of a small

company down on its luck. The floor was terrazzo, and the furniture looked as if it had been left over after a tag sale. A few photographs of trains could have saved the day, at least as far as I was concerned, but hanging on the walls instead were bland collages. Passengers who would be riding the Acela hurried in and out, with cell phones grafted to their ears and designer bags slung over their shoulders. Beginning fifteen minutes or so before each Acela departure, the waiting room would begin to fill, like a tide pool, then empty when the train was called.

I soon realized that a group, perhaps twenty in all, remained each time after the others left. These passengers did not carry cell phones or expensive bags. One woman had a walker; another, with platinum hair, was wearing gold high heels and a lavender wool suit. A family of five included a man in his eighties. This group was waiting for the *Silver Meteor,* and we had little in common with the upscale patrons of the Acela. In fact, we had little in common with one another, except perhaps that we had time to spare. We were going to need it.

I sat where I could watch the electronic board behind the reception desk, and moments before I expected to see our gate posted, "Delayed" flashed up instead. We were informed that our train was in the Sunnyside Yards, which I knew was in Queens, about ten minutes from the station. We would be told the moment the train left the yards and was "in the tunnel" under the East River. Our receptionist was cheerful. Train 97, the *Silver Meteor,* would surely be "in the tunnel" momentarily.

An hour passed, then another. After three hours, we were told that dinner would not be served in the dining car aboard the train as had been planned; instead, it would be delivered to our compartments, in boxes. As for what was wrong out there in the Sunnyside Yards, no one knew, and word that it was still snowing (brought to us by the porters, who were in touch with the conductors aboard other trains) was not encouraging.

At ten-thirty, it was conceded that no dinner would be served aboard. It was hinted that the dining car itself was responsible for the delay. Presently a porter arrived with a large cardboard box, which he placed in the middle of the room. With a gesture that began as a flourish but wound up as a shrug, he indicated that the contents, cold sandwiches, were for us.

Finally, news came that repairs had been completed. The train was "in the tunnel" at eleven thirty-five, and fifteen minutes later, we were ushered aboard. This was what I had been waiting for: the privacy of my own tiny compartment (it measured about seven by three and a half feet), the comfort of the seat, the heft of a good book in my lap, and, close at hand, a large can of Foster's, which I had presciently acquired during the delay. Orlando was 1,124 miles away, according to the timetable. To get there, we would ride rails that Emerson once called "a magician's rod."

At midnight we were under way, and a few moments later we began boring down under the Hudson River. Yellow lights on the walls of the tunnel flashed by every two seconds, marking our speed. I knew we were beyond the river when the train canted upward, but the tunnel ran on, now under the New Jersey Palisades. The yellow lights flared and faded, flared and faded, the abstraction of the interval between them the only indication of our speed. (If some mischievous designer had spaced them progressively closer, I would have assumed the train was accelerating.) Suddenly the lights were gone, we were out of the tunnel, and in this different kind of darkness I could just make out the swampy flatlands of Bergen County.

The train swung through a left turn, the wheel flanges slamming against the inside of the rails. The whistle blew for the first time, a long blast as if the locomotive had been holding its breath.

I looked over my shoulder toward the lights of the city and was startled that they seemed so far away. Having driven in and out of New York many times, I was thrilled to have come this far from it and to have crossed the moatlike Hudson in just five minutes. I was seeing the Empire State Building from the side, as you rarely do in Manhattan. It looked exceptionally slender, somehow vulnerable. The south end of the island, which used to be anchored by the twin shafts of the World Trade Center, now tapered into the night. I looked ahead and could just make out the heavy steel trusses of the Pulaski Skyway, whose concrete piers seemed to be wading through the marshes of the Passaic River.

Traffic on the New Jersey Turnpike paced the train. BUCKLE UP read a billboard. I felt a delightful lightness. No belts here! Seventy mph, and I could move around and stand up. I couldn't see where we were going, but so what? It was great to be tearing through the night without the anxiety that accompanied flying or the responsibilities that went with driving.

In my compartment, the ceiling was the underside of a bunk bed. A sink folded into the wall, and the toilet was disguised as a table. The window was like a camera lens, and I registered the passing sights as if I were a roll of film. *Newark:* the platform glistening with melted ice. *Click! The Raritan River:* lacquered slate beneath a mist of light rain. *Click! Click!* The train was an intruder, hurrying past apartment windows and across back-yards. I was seeing the slums, not the fresh face that towns wear for people driving cars, who might be tempted into stopping.

I had the timetable open in my lap and was penciling in revisions to reflect our late start when we glided into Philadelphia's 30th Street Station. One thirty-seven A.M.; we were there right on the minute that we had been scheduled to arrive, and I reveled in the precision of matching a place to the abstraction of a schedule—setting aside that we happened to be five hours late.

Cities are hard to identify from planes, and from cars you're lucky to glimpse a distant skyline from the ring road. But the train takes you downtown, and stops. Even if it's just for a moment, you are truly *in* Trenton or Philadelphia. Our stops, however, were brief, and I looked forward to Washington, where we were scheduled to be for half an hour; I planned to get off and walk around. But soon after Baltimore I finished the Foster's and was suddenly so tired I climbed up into the bunk and fell asleep. When I woke up, we were already in Washington, stopped by the station platform, and I was too drowsy to bother getting dressed.

I was struck by how quiet it was. No sounds came from the train, and I couldn't hear anything from outside. Looking through the window, I saw two conductors standing together, talking, their breath white. One of them held a rolled-up newspaper, which from time to time he smacked soundlessly against his thigh. A strand of bulbs of the kind you see at construction sites cast a weak, yellowish light onto rusting steel posts. An escalator ran silently, its metal steps vanishing upward into the darkness. A boxy electric locomotive, an AEM-7 that had brought us down from New York, slipped by two tracks away, the slogan A SAFE TEAM ON TIME stenciled on its nose. I heard a bell ringing, faintly. Our new engine, a diesel, was backing into position. *Thunk*.

We crept across the Potomac, then arced around to the left as we came back on land. Picking up speed, we ran parallel to Washington National Airport, with Interstate 87 between us and the runways. For a moment the rails, the road, the runways, and the river formed a stratified geology of transportation. Soon afterward, as we rolled through Alexandria, I fell asleep again.

While I slept, the *Silver Meteor* passed three major battlefields of the Civil War: Manassas, Fredericksburg, and Petersburg, going by them in the exact chronological order in which these bloody battles had been fought.

Manassas (July 1861), a victory for the South, was the first large-scale confrontation of the war, and it was fought before either side was really organized. Fredericksburg, a year and a half later, belonged to the the war's middle period, when the armies were experienced, professional, and evenly matched. It, too, went to the Confederates, now commanded by Lee. But by the time the war reached Petersburg (June 1864), Lee had lost at Gettysburg, and the Union's Army of the Potomac, recently placed under Grant's command, had gained the upper hand. Entrenched around Petersburg, the two adversaries stared at each other until spring 1865, when Grant succeeded in forcing Lee out of his position. Lee began a retreat to the west, with Grant in hot pursuit. The ninety miles from Petersburg to Appomattox, where Grant caught up, were the final miles of the war.

They were also the first miles of a journey for thousands of young men who would continue on from Appomattox to Council Bluffs and Omaha, where they hooked up with the work crews who were just beginning to build the Transcontinental Railroad. By early summer 1865, just weeks after the end of the Civil War, men still wearing blue and gray uniforms were working side by side hefting rails and driving spikes.

A few of these men, by then in their late thirties and early forties, would help construct the Midland.

From the trenches of Petersburg to trestle building on the High Line—it can't have been easy. But what a life.

My bunk was close to the top of the car, and when the whistle blew the sound seemed to roll back along the roof of the train and over my head. When dawn came, we were crossing through a swamp. I was still lying down, so the roots and branches and reflected light all seemed to be rushing up from my feet. Half asleep, I felt weightless, as if I were hurtling through space. At nine-fifteen, we were slowing for Rocky Mount, the first stop in North Carolina. I dressed as we paused at the station, and started down the corridor toward the dining car just as we were pulling out.

The train lurched and bucked as it gathered speed along the rough roadbed. In the corridors, I ricocheted along like a pinball, dodging the embrace of the platinum-haired woman I had noticed the night before. In the dining car, you sat wherever a seat was available, and I wound up with two members of a Canadian family, the husband and his daughter. He was embarrassed to be taking the train and explained to me that it was only because his wife's father was afraid of planes. Our breakfasts arrived, delivered by a waiter who, like those I remembered from my trips as a kid, was a showman, an accomplished equilibrist who would amble down the aisle with a loaded tray held aloft, defying the jarring ride with practiced ease.

By the time I was back in my compartment, we were well into North Carolina. Scrub pines were shrouded in a mouse-gray murk. Run-down houses were pulled up close to the rails as if the people who lived in them hoped they might someday be scooped up by a passing train and taken to a better world. In the towns, warehouses, factories, and mills drifted by the window, industries that were once the soul of the country, nurtured by the trains. No more.

Eleven A.M.; the pace was slower, less urgent. Sunday morning. Backyards were filled with trash and old cars. No laundry lines these days; everyone now owns a washer/dryer. The whistle blew the same four blasts, taking fifteen seconds from first to last, for everything from deserted sandy lanes to paved roads crowded with churchgoers (flowers in the women's hats and purses in their laps) waiting in their cars for the train to pass.

I imagined us as seen from above, a silver line moving through a landscape that had started out gray, was now reddish brown, and would turn green in the little bit of daylight that would be left when we reached northern Florida.

Lunch. Each table had been set with a small vase of artificial flowers, and a strengthening sun made ours glow. I was sitting across from a couple who said they had boarded at Philadelphia and were, like me, headed for Orlando. They were heavily tatooed. Vipers and serpents ran along their forearms, seeming to reach out for their food. He was pale and mild, she was dark, with a husky voice and hair spilling over her shoulders. Like the man from Toronto, they took pains to justify their presence on the train, as if trains (like buses) were now acceptable only for the very old, or for those who, somehow, were so down on their luck as not to own a car.

We were now seven hours behind schedule. We had lost our right-of-way and frequently pulled onto sidings to let other trains, including freights, go by. (John Pryke and Tony Koester would have loved this!) I figured that unless Casey Jones himself arose from the grave to take over the controls, we would be lucky to arrive much before midnight. Everyone around me in the dining car was cheerful, however, and no cell phones were being used to change plans.

Charleston. Yemassee. Savannah. As evening approached, the shadow of our train grew bolder in its flirtations with the passing landscape, sliding down the slope into a water-filled ditch, reaching across a field to darken the side of a barn, then jumping back to the safety of the nearby undergrowth, where pixilated fragments of greens, browns, and tans rushed by close to the window. The sounds, even the whistle, had become so familiar that I was no longer aware of hearing them, and I was startled by a sudden hollow roaring; I looked up from my book to see the girders of a bridge scissoring by, with a tidal estuary spreading out beyond. The sun went behind clouds before it set, and the marshes turned gunmetal gray, then black.

Jacksonville. I stepped off onto the platform, and my legs, which by now had grown accustomed to the movement of the train, felt shaky. The night air was warm. The conductors and porters went through the motions of hustling to unload the passengers and their bags, as if the idea of clawing back even a few minutes of the lost time still mattered.

We began to move again, and the train's headlight hollowed out a hole in the darkness, which we slipped through, leaving the night to fill the void behind us. The window, which had been a lens, now reflected only the inside of the compartment, an eye turned in upon itself. A blinking eye: the reading lamp was failing, flickering on and off at random. According to the timetable, the last thirty-seven miles from DeLand to Orlando would take more than an hour and a quarter—and the last few miles would be traversed at little more than 10 mph. Like Zeno, or an aging marathon runner, the closer we came to the finish line, the slower we went.

When we reached the outskirts of Orlando, I took my bag and went to the forward end of the car. The Canadian family, the tattooed couple, and a dozen others were there, too, and we crowded together in the vestibule, our bags at our feet. The *Silver Meteor* eased along at walking speed, like a cruise ship maneuvering toward a dock. In contrast to our stately pace, the whistle had become frantic, each quartet of notes barely finished before beginning again. The tracks ran diagonally through the grid of streets, and level crossings came every block. The lights of the waiting cars shone on the damp pavement, turning it gold. The air was thick and hot; I smelled fresh-cut grass. In a tidy backyard, a pair of pink plastic flamingos were standing in a flower bed.

I was in the parking lot renting a car when the *Silver Meteor* pulled out. One moment it was there, a stainless-steel curtain behind an arcade of stucco arches, but when I looked up after signing the contract, it was gone. This train had a ghostly quality from the start, I decided. Hiding in the Sunnyside Yards. Slipping through the crowded Northeast corridor at night. Falling so far behind schedule as to have vanished from the screens at Centralized Traffic Control. Forty years ago, people would wave from their backyards or from cars waiting at level crossings, but today when we went by they seemed to stare right through the train.

Still, Amtrak reports an encouraging increase in the number of passengers riding the *Silver Meteor.* In one month (April 2003), it was a 27 percent jump from the year before (to 26,000). But many of Amtrak's trains operate in the red, and their future cannot be assured. It is clear that this country's long-distance trains no longer play the essential role in public transportation they once did. Yet I hope they can survive. Perhaps trains like the *Silver Meteor,* in addition to connecting places, will come to be valued as time machines, linking us with the past. On that level, these long-distance trains are winners, an authentic way of experiencing history. For $287 (the cost of my ticket, New York to

Orlando, one way), you not only get somewhere, you see history out the window as you go. The tracks take you through the heart of our gritty industrial heritage, places you can no longer see from a car, while in rural areas the presence of the tracks themselves has kept progress at bay. You see the past mirrored in the aging faces of the men and women who run the trains, and you feel it in the train's pace, which was once considered breathtakingly fast but most of the time is just too slow and labored for our modern taste.

Tourist trains dispense with the obligation of providing conventional transportation and instead offer passengers a combination of nostalgia (in the form of vintage steam locomotives) and scenery. Colorado's Durango-and-Silverton narrow gauge railroad exploits this formula as well as anyone. It uses charismatic eighty-year-old steamers to haul upward of 200,000 passengers annually through the spectacular Animas River Gorge, which is inaccessible by automobile.

Another successful tourist line (400,000 visitors per year) is located in the rolling farmland of southeastern Pennsylvania. Called the Strasburg Rail Road, it operates a superb roster of standard gauge steam locomotives, along with fully restored passenger cars reeking of Victorian elegance.

Soon after my ride on the *Silver Meteor,* I was going to Strasburg. But I wouldn't be buying a ticket. I was going to be taught how to drive the train.

The idea was that I would "test" a locomotive for *Road & Track* magazine, which each spring publishes what they call their April Fool's road test. Through the years, they have sampled a wide variety of unusual conveyances, including the Goodyear Blimp, Budweiser's beer wagon, the *QE2,* the Concord, and an

Iditarod sled. They tested an aristocratic English locomotive, a Gresley A3 Pacific, back in 1966; now, almost forty years later, it seemed like the right moment for another locomotive test, only this time it would be an American engine, Strasburg's No. 90, a 1924 Baldwin.

I was excited about going to Strasburg. The Baldwin had been built in the heyday of steam, and since I regarded steam locomotives as the most romantic objects in railroad history, to drive one—to *control* it—would surely bring me full circle on that journey I began back in my Lionel days.

POWERED BY STEAM

I arrived at the Strasburg Rail Road's engine house, which closely resembled John Allen's model, at six o'clock on a freakishly hot August morning (it was already over eighty degrees). A storm threatened in the distance, a gray sky meeting the intense green of fields planted with maize.

As hot as it was outside, it was even hotter inside. Steam engines are not turned off at the end of the day; the fire in their fireboxes is kept burning around the clock. When I stood close to the four locomotives crowded into Strasburg's engine house, it was hard to see them as inanimate machines. A young mechanic (known as a "hostler") was preparing the two engines that would be in action when the railroad opened for business at 11 A.M. As he stoked their fires, the pressure in their boilers began to rise, accompanied by the *ping!* and *bah!* of expanding steel. Sweat ran down the sides of the engines, beading on the hot, greasy metal. Air brakes chatted to themselves in rapid bursts of clicks and thunks. Steam escaped (*pissssiitt!*) at random intervals and from places that took me by surprise. I made the mistake of leaving my briefcase open on the floor, and moments later it was soaking wet.

The first steam engines were developed in England in the early eighteenth century to operate pumps in mines, and soon they were adapted to provide power for boats. The first crude locomotives followed, and by 1860 powerful, reliable steam engines were commonplace.

Although steam is simple to produce—just boil water—it has protean characteristics that can be exploited to generate staggering amounts of energy. Water turning to steam expands to 1,600 times its original volume. In a locomotive that expansion is contained, or trapped. Trying to expand, but having limited space to do so, the steam instead becomes denser. Pressure builds.

The water is heated when it comes in contact with over 200 small-diameter tubes stretching the full length of the boiler. Running through these tubes are hot gasses (2,500 degrees Fahrenheit) from the firebox. The steam rising off the top of the water in the boiler is already hot (390 degrees), but it undergoes a second round of heating in an apparatus aptly called a superheater. The superheater raises the temperature of the steam to more than 600 degrees—and also dries it out, which gives it a greater concentration of energy when it is released into the cylinders. There, like a man who has been stuck in a closet finding that he can open the door, the steam expands, pushing the piston. Because the piston is connected to the locomotive's wheels by a system of rods and cranks, the wheels must move, too.

When the original locomotives were built 170 years ago, the sight of fire, water, and steel acting together to produce movement was like sorcery. The steam locomotive was the first complex machine that many people, especially those in rural areas, had ever encountered, and for the timid it must have been an alarming experience. Billowing clouds of smoke. The shriek of the whistle. The connecting rods thrashing like the legs of a galloping horse. The ground trembling. A locomotive could appear from nowhere and be on top of you faster than you could think.

The Strasburg Rail Road's No. 90 was built in Philadelphia by the Baldwin Locomotive Works, which had also produced the Midland's engines. Baldwin was America's longest-lived (1832–1956) and most prolific steam engine builder. No. 90 had been a freight locomotive before coming to Strasburg, hauling sugar beets on the Colorado plains. It was neither fast nor particularly powerful, but to me No. 90 had everything a classic steam engine should have: a long boiler, a sturdy smokestack, plenty of wheels, and enough pipes, valves, grease fittings, and unidentifiable gizmos to make it look exceedingly rugged and purposeful. It had a hooded headlight and a brass bell. Its cylinders hung low, like Churchillian jowls. Except for gold numbers and trim, plus a red-roofed cab, No. 90 was all black.

I was up in the cab with the hostler when he backed the engine outside to a loading dock, where he used a bucket loader to put coal in the tender. It had begun to rain, and white lines slanted across the maize, as in a Chinese woodcut. Smoke drifted forward from the stack, a vaporous gray dissolving in the stormy sky. The cab was three-sided, with the back totally open to the rain, but the engine's heat acted as an invisible shield, keeping me dry. The boiler thrust into the cab from the front. It was overgrown with a tangle of pipes and gauges, most of them too hot to touch. The throttle was a three-foot-long steel bar that projected back from the boiler at shoulder height. The firebox doors snapped open, jawlike, and I could see past them to a carpet of flame. The smell was of rain and damp earth, mingling with coal and hot grease.

My chance to drive No. 90 came early the next day. The hostler, Chuck Trusdell, took me out onto the Strasburg's main line, stopped the engine, and stepped away from the controls. Ever since getting my hands on Lionel's ZW, I had sought out machines that would give me something for nothing: cars that sprang into action with the slightest pressure on the accelerator, boats that swept through the water with the wind in their sails. Now here I was with 1,700 horsepower on tap, with enough tractive power to pull twenty loaded cars. During the night, the boiler pressure had been a relaxed, slow-breathing 80 pounds per square inch. Now it was 250, and No. 90 felt taut, expectant, up on its toes. *Ping!* The day before, I had made several runs with the regular engineer and fireman, so I was familiar with the vibration, the noise, the soot, and the way the engine slammed from side to side, as if it was trying to leap clear of the rails.

The fields around us were owned by Amish farmers, and nearby one was cutting the maize with a horse-drawn harvester. Neither man nor horse looked up. They were trying to live in a world in which our iron horse represented the future, whereas to me the steam engine was linked irrevocably with the past. The year No. 90 was built, 1924, cars had progressed only as far as Ford's Model T, and in aviation the news was the completion of the first round-the-world flight, in fifteen days.

The time had come. I closed the cylinder cocks and released the brakes. Then I reached for the throttle bar.

While the actual acceleration of a vehicle powered by steam may be similar to one with an internal combustion engine, the sensation is different. The steam engine—or steam car—glides forward effortlessly, as if it were weightless. The accompanying sound (*chuufffhh*) is an exhalation, ending almost in a sigh. Internal combustion engines, by contrast, have to be revved up in order to generate power, and you can sense them girding for the effort, like a sprinter going into a crouch. With steam, the throttle releases power that is *already there*. I suddenly understood the far-away look I had seen in engineers' eyes. The power they had on tap could get them to the horizon. They felt drawn forward, not pushed.

I made several runs back and forth along a short straight, enjoying myself immensely but in real railroading terms not even scratching the surface of what it would be like to be making a serious run, against the clock, out on the main line. I didn't dream of being an engineer in the Lionel days, but my few minutes driving No. 90 convinced me I had missed something. Here was much the same feeling that had attracted me to design and racing, which are both about the creation, and then the distribution, of force.

Consider the delicate balance between power and traction. Starting up, or lugging a heavy freight on a hill, a locomotive's driving wheels may suddenly lose traction and spin wildly. They say the best engineers can feel it coming, either through experience or hypersensitivity to a slight vibration in the frame, and ease off the throttle, or quickly release some sand in front of the driving wheels, for extra grip. You can also try slamming the throttle shut, then instantly reopen it—and sometimes the wheels will catch.

Owing to the enormous momentum of a train, it is often necessary to begin braking long before you can see what you are braking for, and I would have enjoyed judging my shutoff points for distant curves or bridges. I would have liked to feel the pulse of a locomotive, keeping my eye on its pressures and temperatures, figuring out, moment to moment, how best to let it do its work, being stingy with coal and water while still making time. I would have enjoyed the camaraderie with the fireman, the two of us communicating through the medium of the machine.

Every run in the age of steam was different: no two engines were just the same, the loads were dissimilar, and the weather was variable. The engineer's job was to achieve the optimum resolution of all of these vectored forces. He also had to be a human stopwatch. Being *on time* was, in a sense, railroading's catechism, the question posed by the timetable, the answer in the hands of the train crew. A train operating on time was part of the smoothly functioning machinery of the nation. A train running late was somehow a threat to that. But a late train *making up time,* racing through a rainy night, stirred the imagination, to the point that foolish risks were countenanced, even praised.

Steam locomotives, for all their tough steel construction, fiery interiors, and brutish demeanor, were innately vulnerable. They were hopelessly complex, at least for their time. A classification system developed in 1900 by a New York Central mechanical engineer named Frederick M. Whyte lists thirty-two possible wheel arrangements, from yard switchers to over-the-road freight haulers. The *Locomotive Encyclopedia of America* names almost 350 major parts per engine. Since the railroads ordered locomotives in small quantities and then customized them not long after delivery, no two would be alike either in specification or the way they ran. In addition to requiring hard-to-get parts (few being standardized), steam locomotives demanded around-the-clock maintenance by expert crews. The head of the Strasburg operation, Linn Moedinger, served an apprenticeship under a Pennsylvania Railroad boilermaker, and Linn, along with a handful of others scattered around the country, is one of the few young people to have been taught by the last generation of railroaders who ran steam. Linn told me that while some of what he knows is conceptual, and therefore can be written down and passed along, much is intuitive—or so specific to a particular engine that it can be acquired only by working alongside someone with years of experience. Such men are still alive, in their seventies and eighties, but it's easy to see that much of what must be known to keep engines like No. 90 running will soon be gone. Recently, Linn advertised free classes in locomotive maintenance, and only one person showed up.

Steam engines weren't cheap to operate. Suppose you wished to run one just twenty miles. No. 90, a medium-sized locomotive, would consume a ton of coal (all of it shoveled into the firebox by hand) and 1,700 gallons of water. The tender's capacity limits the cruising range to one hundred miles, which means the railroads had to maintain an expensive network of water towers and coaling stations. Turntables were required to get the locomotives pointed in the right direction, and roundhouses were needed to protect them from the weather. Their boilers had to be cleaned after every thirty hours of operation.

If neglected, steam engines had a disturbing tendency to blow themselves up. When the fireman, or the hostler, or whoever was in charge let the water level in the boiler run low, the top of the crown sheet (the roof of the firebox) would be exposed and become red hot. At the first contact with a fresh supply of cool water—*boom!* The boiler would launch itself forward like a clumsy rocket, tearing clear of the frame as it went. Records document boiler parts weighing up to ten tons being flung as far as one thousand feet. Smaller shrapnel might go a half mile. The blast usually pitched what was left of the engine onto its side, derailing several cars behind it. The exploding locomotive had a way of taking its revenge upon those who had neglected it: almost every time, the engineer or fireman—or both—would be killed.

Another reason steam locomotives were feared by trainmen was that in a wreck, steam lines would break, often scalding the crew—a nightmarish way to die, even if you were lucky enough to die fast. Train crews so feared being trapped in the cab that when they saw a crash coming they would try to leap clear, no matter how fast they were going. With a touch of gallows humor, this was called "joining the birds."

Some locomotives were thought to be jinxed. In 1887, the Colorado Midland purchased seven ostensibly identical locomotives, but one—Engine No. 22—was destined to behave very differently than the others. The Morris Cafky book lists its misadventures, starting with a series of harmless derailments. Then No. 22 turned bad, accelerating out of a siding and smashing into a passing excursion train. The locomotive's steam lines ruptured, and eleven passengers were scalded to death. In the next two years, No. 22 flipped twice, killing the fireman both times. Its next crash was head-on into a Denver & Rio Grande passenger train. Fire broke out; sixteen people died. The "hoodoo engine," as it had become known, was rebuilt in time to run into yet another Denver & Rio Grande train. This time, No. 22 got the worst of it. The impact shoved the locomotive backward over its own tender (killing the fireman). Another head-on followed, then a collision in which No. 22 rear-ended a stationary train. A wreck caused by the collapse of a burning trestle, and an unexplained derailment while puttering around a yard, closed out the malevolent No. 22's Midland career.

The basic technical development of steam locomotives was over by 1920. After that, it was just a question of refinement and that last resort of any stagnant technology: making things bigger. The climax of this trend came in the early 1940s with the Union Pacific Railroad's aptly named Big Boys, which had 6,000 horsepower and weighed close to four hundred tons.

Steam's last chapter was written in the 1950s, in the Appalachian Mountains of western Virginia. It was documented by O. Winston Link, a photographer with a background in advertising. Link had been fascinated by trains since his childhood, and when he realized steam's days were numbered, he wrote the Norfolk and Western, one of the last major railroads using steam power. They agreed to allow him full access to railroad property and sometimes even modified their schedules to help him get the shots he wanted.

Eighty years before, William Henry Jackson had photographed trains in the exuberant era of Western expansion. Now Link was producing an elegy. He shot in black and white, at night, using elaborate synchronized-flash effects to illuminate the train and certain carefully chosen surroundings. In one shot, an elderly couple sit on a porch as a train rushes by behind them. In another, taken at a drive-in theater, a young man and his date snuggle in the front seat of a convertible while a train races out from behind the screen. In a third, a man holding an ax and a Christmas tree stands with his son, who waves as a locomotive thunders over a stone bridge.

Link's engines evoked power and speed, pouring white smoke into the black night and trailing steam from their cylinders. But he photographed them as a part of everyday life, managing in picture after picture to convey a sense of imminent loss, suggesting that with their passing something grand would be gone from the lives of people who lived along the tracks.

The Norfolk and Western clung to steam until 1960—longer than any other major American railroad. It made sense for them in a way it didn't for other railroads. The area they served produced coal, and labor in the hill towns of Virginia and West Virginia was cheap. In other parts of the world where similar conditions existed, steam engines also survived. In the 1980s, they could be seen hauling sugarcane in the Philippines, or carrying freight in Mombassa, or transporting passengers across the desolate plains of the Pakistan Punjab. In China, steam remained dominant deep into the 1990s, with great red-wheeled monsters crawling up the Jingpeng Pass, two hundred miles north of Beijing.

The demise of the steam locomotive began in 1935 with the appearance of the diesel. Diesels were down-to-earth and undemanding—and they had powerful allies. Diesels consumed oil, not coal, so the oil companies lobbied for them. Most diesels were built by General Motors and General Electric, industrial giants with plenty of capital to invest in the new technology. GM and GE were accustomed to mass production, and from the beginning they discouraged the railroads' desire to customize the design and tinker with the finished product. In return, the railroads were guaranteed a reliable machine that ran forever between overhauls and for which spare parts were always available. And all the early diesels were *streamlined*.

The year 1935 marked the zenith of American infatuation with streamlining. Intended as an antidote to the Depression, streamlined products were designed to suggest the future instead of the past. Uncluttered lines. Curves. Organic form. Frank Lloyd Wright rounded off the corners of the Johnson's Wax Building, Hoover made its vacuum cleaner in the shape of a bullet. Radios, telephones, and even sewing machines were given the treatment. Most of the new design was pure illusion and marketing (streamlining a refrigerator didn't make it keep your milk any colder), but that didn't dampen public enthusiasm for the Look. However, areas of design did exist where slippery, aerodynamically correct shapes actually could boost performance. Airplanes, certainly, and automobiles.

Trains also seemed to be an ideal subject for streamlining. Even before the debut of the diesels, railroads had commissioned artists and engineers to make concept drawings, but nothing was ever built. Then the first diesel streamliner appeared, and you could almost hear the sound of designers sharpening their pencils. The New York Central hired an earnest young aerodynamicist named Norman Zapf, who conducted wind-tunnel tests and produced a metal sheath that enclosed the wheels and eliminated all ladders, grab rails, and external piping. It resembled an inverted bathtub. Meanwhile, the Milwaukee Road chose an industrial designer, Otto Kuhler, who drew a slightly more stylish version of Zapf's bathtub and embellished it with a lively color scheme. Then Raymond Loewy joined the game on behalf of the Pennsylvania Railroad and took the lead by combining the science of aerodynamics with a stylist's touch.

Other designers caught on and soon styling was the only concern. If it looked sleek, it got the green light. Otto Kuhler, by then on board with the Lehigh Valley Railroad, introduced delicate horizontal fins that seemed to slice the air. Henry Dreyfuss's design for the New York Central's *20th Century Limited* was a bullet nose bisected by a thick vertical fin that recalled the helmet of a Roman charioteer. With each fresh iteration, designers exposed more and more of the wheels and drivers, both for practicality (it was highly inconvenient for mechanics to unbolt the heavy metal shrouds every time an engine needed servicing) and also because they had come to recognize the visceral power of all those pumping rods and whirling wheels. The ladders, grab rails, and external piping began to reappear. Norfolk and Western's J-class streamliner didn't cover the wheels at all, and Southern Pacific's Daylight series, probably the most popular streamliners ever, were basically standard engines with a silver nose and little more "streamlining" than a flat orange panel running down their sides.

But not one of these locomotives ever looked as truly modern as an ordinary diesel right out of the box. A steam engine was suddenly old (you just *felt* it), and when the railroads attempted to pander to public taste through styling, they only made matters worse. For more than a century, the design of steam locomotives had existed outside the realm of public judgment because they were understood to be the products of pure engineering and not subject to fads or changes of taste. Their beauty wasn't skin deep—it came from deep inside, from the Promethean mysteries of fire.

Many steam engines had such personality that stories abound of grown men crying as they watched a favorite locomotive heading for the wrecking yard. The locomotive, its boiler fires having been extinguished, would be towed to a siding. There, a few reusable parts, such as the bell and the gauges, were removed the way a convicted man about to enter jail surrenders his wallet and belt. Then the wreckers would go to work, hacking off the sand dome, the smokestack, and sections of the cab. A welder with an acetylene torch flayed the side of the boiler, exposing the fire tubes, and then the tubes were cut apart, clattering as they fell down across the wheels. Other sounds were the *whoosh* of the torch, the dull *whuung* of sledgehammers breaking up rivets, the *thud* of heavy parts hitting the ground.

Only a handful of locomotives have escaped. Most of them are in museums or town squares, as static displays. To see one in operation has become a treat, and to have driven one is a rare privilege. In our basement, of course, the trains ran anytime we wanted them to—and my recent outing aboard No. 90 allowed me to attach my memories of the real thing to our little locomotives, making them—in my eyes—more fascinating than ever and drawing me into a world that was neither 1:1 nor 1:87, but somehow both.

E P I L O G U E

The annual railroad hobby show at the Eastern States Exposition Grounds, in Springfield, Massachusetts, was scheduled for early February. John and I had gone to the show when he was ten, and now, ten years later, we planned to go again. He would drive down from Maine, where he was at college, and we would meet midafternoon.

I went early and arrived at 1 P.M. I was directed to a parking spot on the perimeter of the lot, which was nearly full. The line at the ticket booth was long, and when I eventually made my way into the main exhibition hall it was jammed. I found Rolf at his exhibit, which consisted of a pair of tables piled to shoulder level with boxes of used trains. He offered me a chair. Rolf first exhibited here in 1980, and I kidded him about taking the booth more to see his friends (a steady stream came by to say hello) than to sell trains. He just laughed. "What is all this old stuff, anyhow?" I asked.

"It's not *old stuff*—those are *collector's* items," he said, grinning. From where we sat behind the pile of boxes, I could watch people as they walked past. Most had taken the opportunity, in some aspect of their attire, to declare themselves as members of the culture of model railroading. One couple wore engineer's hats; his had blue and white stripes, hers pink and white. Jackets covered with railroad logos were popular, as were T-shirts with detailed renderings of locomotives. I saw a miniature level-crossing signal (with flashing red lights) worn on a man's lapel. But the true believer's signature article of clothing was a vest literally armored with enameled pins. Add a beard and you had all options covered. Physical infirmities were no obstacle to attendance. One man was being wheeled from exhibit to exhibit on a gurney. Another was breathing oxygen from a portable tank.

As for me, my right hand soon began to shake. I left Rolf and went to a concession stand, where I bought a Coke and took the pills that my doctor prescribes. The nightmarish scenarios I had envisioned during those first weeks after discovering I had Parkinson's have yet to occur. In my case—and I have been lucky—the disease has advanced slowly, and the arsenal of drugs available to fight it is growing all the time.

It was 3 P.M., and I thought that John must be almost here. He and I had talked recently of other layouts that might be fun to build. The Nullarbor Straight? Maybe there was a way, after all: a continuous belt, or perhaps a giant drum, painted like the desert, geared to turn at the speed of the locomotive, so it could run the full three hundred scale miles without moving, relative to the room. We thought of modeling the trestle that linked Boca Grande to the mainland, with twenty feet of azure blue water in the foreground blending seamlessly at the horizon into a sky that exactly matched the water. We thought of creating a hillside, with real dirt, that would fill Ellen's whole studio, then having it professionally surveyed and engineering a route for a single track that would take a train from the bottom to the top, a climb of fourteen feet.

Any big layout has a life of its own. In the four years since ours was essentially finished, I have wondered: Is it a toy? Not exactly. A piece of furniture? No. A work of art? Not in the way I think of art. It is probably most accurately described as a representation, or manifestation, of a certain amount of work. The question I am most often asked is, How long did it take to build? The answer—six thousand hours—seems to satisfy some but mystify others. I see it as a finite portion of my life, measuring sixteen years from start to finish, and if I'm in a gloomy mood it worries me that the time passed so quickly. Add sixteen years to my current age, and I'm an old man!

The layout doesn't appear to be aging at all. The Plexiglas has protected it well. Rolf did such a good job with the wiring and the track that the trains still run smoothly and without derailing. A couple of the buildings have cracked at the corners, where the glue has dried and become brittle, but I'm the only one who seems to have noticed. Eventually, the colors of the rocks and trees will begin to fade, but so far they remain bright.

Having kids over is the most fun. They like to crawl underneath and bob up in the openings that are hidden in the mountains—it's as if they are suddenly backstage at the theater. The trains switch identities, too: when they're out of sight back in the world of unpainted plywood, they are like actors in costume waiting for the curtain to go up. One area near the middle, where a mountain ridge hides the tracks, is virtually inaccessible, but since no train has ever stalled or derailed along that stretch, I haven't had to go back there for years. I've wondered what the locomotives' headlights illuminate as the trains come through: cobwebs, I would think, and forgotten tools, perhaps a dead mouse.

Visitors are intrigued by the wrecked locomotive, which appears to have pitched down an embankment. Although we originally installed it just for the second *Model Railroader* article, Rolf and I liked the way it recalled the misadventures of the Midland's No. 22—and, invariably, after hearing the stories, someone will ask, "So, when did *this* wreck occur?" The factory at Newman's Own continues to pollute, and the ongoing Ping-Pong game on the loading dock is evidence that the company's management couldn't care less. As new products have been tested, the number of gravestones out behind the factory has doubled.

Next year, we're planning an open house for a division of the National Model Railroad Association. Rolf is going to build skylights for the roundhouse so the members can see inside to the locomotives—and I hope to get some of them wired for sound. *Ssssis. Thunk. Shhhhhhuuh . . .*

We have a new digital camera that we set up on the layout where bigger cameras won't fit, and it has made shots from places no one has ever seen before (and exposed some unfinished parts that I plan to work on).

Ellen says she senses a revival. . . .

Three-thirty. I left the cafeteria and resumed my walk through the show, keeping an eye out for John. Prices ranged from ten cents for old postcards to $4,000 for a completed textile mill that sported the sort of detailing you would expect of George Sellios. The Federal Railroad Administration's booth featured the warning "Always Expect a Train." (Obviously, they hadn't heard of the *Silver Meteor.*) At another booth, you could buy a plaque that read: LIONEL TRAINS ONLY; ALL OTHERS WILL BE DERAILED. A vendor hoping to appeal to women had quilts and dresses for sale, with railroad motifs. No takers. It was slow going, too, at an educational exhibit devoted to the history of milk trains in New England.

The stars of the show were the dozen or so layouts that model railroading clubs had on display. A club layout worked this way: Individual members constructed modules (roughly five feet long) that were linked together, usually forming a rectangle with rounded corners. Club members and their wives hung out in the center, with the modules acting as a barrier that protected them from the crowd. It was as if the early settlers had circled their wagons to fend off the Indians. The fancier clubs had matching jackets; my nod for Best Look went to the Quaboag Valley Railroaders, of Albany, New York, who were resplendent in black and silver.

Lionel's display had obviously been designed by professional marketers. In 1985, General Mills sold Lionel to a Detroit real estate man named Richard Kughn, an enthusiast whose love for trains led him to introduce new lines and to sharply upgrade the electronics. In 1995, Kughn sold out to Wellspring Associates, an investment group that included Neil Young, and they have recently moved their production facilities from Michigan to Korea. The all-American toy is no longer all-American. Nonetheless, fathers were pointing out the trains' features to their sons just as if it were half a century ago and they were posing for one of Joshua Cowen's catalogs. The company was about to announce a new HO line. Lionel trains running on two tracks instead of three—I had waited a long time for that! At the exhibit, I noticed that Dad was buying Lionel's trains for himself, not for Son. This paradigm shift may be due to spiraling costs: the new HO locomotives were estimated to be in the $700 range, while a full-size Lionel engine, loaded with sound and DCC, now costs up to $1,500.

I went back to Rolf's exhibit and found him having an animated conversation with John. I was astonished that my son was so much taller than Rolf—but I realized with a shock that it was nearly ten years since the afternoon that Rolf had shown John how the control panel worked, and that was the last time I could remember seeing them together.

Two hours remained before the show would shut down for the day, so John and I hurried excitedly from one exhibit to another. Our best moment came right at closing. An elderly gentleman was standing near his model of the Erie Canal's Lock 17, and he agreed to show us a full working cycle. It had real water, dyed blue, which was surprisingly convincing. I had wanted to see the lock earlier, but it had attracted such large crowds that I couldn't get close. Now we were being treated to a private demonstration.

Finally John had to go. I walked out to the parking lot with him and watched as he drove away. Would he ever build a layout? I didn't think he would until he had his own kids. He is handy with tools and has already built some wooden models as well as a series of real boats; he has the skill, certainly, to pull it off. A second-generation big layout, as far as I know, has not been done, except in the sense that John Allen was a "father" to so many of us.

I wandered back inside for one last look around. One club still had a train running, a trio of diesels slowly pulling a long line of freight cars, around and around. I talked with one of the members, but we were both distracted because we knew the show was over and it was time to go home.

But playing with trains is fun, and for some of us it is awfully hard to stop.

ACKNOWLEDGMENTS

"I like books about obsessions," my editor, Ileene Smith, said to me. "Why not write about building your train layout?" It hadn't occurred to me to think of the layout as an obsession, but as I dug back into what had actually gone on in our basement I began to think she had been right.

She usually is.

When it came to editing the manuscript, Ileene was both warmly enthusiastic and utterly ruthless—in my view, the perfect editor.

Eric Simonoff, my agent at Janklow and Nesbit, was intrigued by his young son's interest in trains, and I hope this book inspires the two of them to get started on a layout.

At *Model Railroader,* Jim Kelly was the first to open the door, and I have felt at home there ever since. Publisher Russ Larson provided statistics, which made me appreciate how big this hobby really is. My special thanks to executive editor Andy Sperandeo; Andy made all the introductions to the modelers I visited, as well as to John Sanheim at the Walthers Company.

The modelers—Ned Swigart, Don Buckley, Dave Townsend, Jim Hediger, Tony Koester, Malcolm Furlow, Dave Frary, Bob Hayden, John Pryke, and George Sellios—welcomed me into their homes and shared their layouts and their experiences with me.

Linn Moedinger, president of the Strasburg Rail Road, gave me one of the great thrills of my life when he let me drive his No. 90 Baldwin steam locomotive. He also showed remarkable patience in trying to educate me in the mysteries of steam.

My family was behind this project from the beginning. My mother helped me recall details from my early layouts. My wife, Ellen, listened each evening for many months to the latest installments. Our son, John, showed as much interest in the book as he had in the layout itself, and he read and reread the manuscript with great care, finding countless places it could be improved. Judy took it upon herself to critique the various titles that were proposed, shooting down one idea after another until we got it right.

Shari Marks, our secretary, did much of the research, and her confidence in computer matters kept me from getting too frazzled when things went wrong. When the gremlins were too much even for Shari, we turned to our guru of electronics, Trish Morrissey, who never failed us.

Nathaniel Sobel took time away from his studies to suggest a useful change to the book's beginning.

The team at Random House has been wonderful. To Gene Mydlowski, Dennis Ambrose, Robin Rolewicz, Carol Schneider, and Erich Schoeneweiss: many thanks.

The quality and variety of books about railroading is amazing. For facts and inspiration I have relied on books as different as David Plowden's sober and thoughtful *A Time of Trains,* Katie Letcher Lyle's lively collection of railroad ballads, *Scalded to Death by the Steam,* and *Stations,* written and superbly illustrated by Michael Flanagan. I also recommend Lucius Beebe's many railroad histories, Vladimir Nabokov's classic account of his childhood trips aboard the Nord-Express, from his autobiography *Speak, Memory,* and Paul Theroux's masterful books on traveling by train.

Lastly, my thanks to all those generations of men and women who have built and operated our country's railroads. We modelers re-create their trains and scenery, but there is no way to re-create their spirit. It just doesn't come in kit form—not even from the Walthers catalog.

SAM POSEY was a professional race car driver for nearly twenty years. His career highlights include a fifth place in the Indianapolis 500 and a win in the Twelve Hours of Sebring. After retiring from the track, Posey became a commentator for ABC, receiving an Emmy Award in Sportswriting for *Trans-Antarctica, the International Expedition.* His first book, *The Mudge Pond Express,* describes his racing days. He lives above his train layout in northwestern Connecticut, with his wife and two children.

ABOUT THE TYPE

This book was set in Granjon, a modern recutting of a typeface produced under the direction of George W. Jones, who based Granjon's design upon the letterforms of Claude Garamond (1480–1561). The name was given to the typeface as a tribute to the typographic designer Robert Granjon.